OPPORT

in

Your Own
Se ice Business

OPPORTUNITIES

in

Your Own
Service Business

REVISED EDITION

ROBERT MCKAY

New York   Chicago   San Francisco   Lisbon   London   Madrid   Mexico City
Milan   New Delhi   San Juan   Seoul   Singapore   Sydney   Toronto

Library of Congress Cataloging-in-Publication Data

McKay, Robert.
    Opportunities in your own service business / by Robert McKay. — Rev. ed.
        p.   cm.
    Includes bibliographical references.
    ISBN 0-07-148210-5 (alk. paper)
    1. Business—Vocational guidance.   2. New business enterprises—Vocational
guidance.   3. Service industries—Management.   I. Title.

    HF5381.M39644   2007
    331.7′93—dc22   2007010425

1 2 3 4 5 6 7 8 9 10 11 12 13 14 15 16 17 18 19   DOC/DOC   0 9 8 7

ISBN 978-0-07-148210-3
MHID   0-07-148210-5

Interior design by Rattray Design

CONTENTS

Introduction

THIS IS AN excellent time to consider starting a service business. The long-term shift from goods-producing to service-producing employment is expected to go on, and service industries will continue to be responsible for most new jobs and businesses in the United States and Canada.

Definition of a Service Business

Webster's dictionary says that service, as we are discussing it here, is "useful labor that does not produce a tangible commodity." In that respect, service businesses can range from those with which you are familiar such as restaurants, grocery and other retail stores, dry cleaners, taxi services, garages, and barber shops to computer service shops, moving companies, airlines, hotels and motels, radio stations, brokerage firms—the list could go on and on.

Before you open your own business, it is a good idea to get some experience by working in the service field that interests you. If you hope to operate your own computer repair business, gaining hands-on experience by working for an established company will be invaluable later on.

Principal Service Businesses

If you are considering starting your own business, you'll want to know where the greatest growth is expected. According to the U.S. Bureau of Labor Statistics, growth through the year 2014 is anticipated as follows:

- **Education and health services.** This sector is expected to add more jobs than any other. In particular, employment in health care and social assistance, including private hospitals, nursing and residential care facilities, and individual and family services will be driven by increasing demand for health care and social assistance because of an aging population and longer life expectancies. Demand for child-care services should grow as more women enter the labor force.
- **Professional and business services.** This sector includes some of the fastest-growing industries in North America. Of these, employment services is expected to exhibit the greatest growth, contributing nearly two-thirds of all new jobs in administrative and support services. Employment in computer systems design should increase based on the growing reliance of businesses on information technology and maintaining system and network security. Rapid growth is also expected in management, scientific, and technical consulting services, spurred by the increased use of new technology and computer software and the growing complexity of business.
- **Information.** Employment in the information sector is expected to add nearly four hundred thousand jobs. Information

contains some of the fast-growing computer-related industries such as software publishing and Internet publishing and broadcasting, as well as Internet service providers, Web search portals, and data processing services. Additional opportunities in this sector include telecommunications, broadcasting, and newspaper, periodical, book, and directory publishers. Increased demand for residential and business land-line and wireless services, cable service, high-speed Internet connections, and software will fuel job growth among these industries.

- **Leisure and hospitality.** Most of the new job openings in this sector will come from the amusement, gambling, and recreation areas. Job growth will stem from public participation in arts, entertainment, and recreation activities, reflecting increasing incomes, leisure time, and awareness of the health benefits of physical fitness. Expansion in the areas of accommodation and food service will be concentrated in eating and drinking establishments, reflecting increases in population, dual-income families, and dining sophistication.

- **Trade, transportation, and utilities.** Transportation and warehousing is expected to add more than five hundred thousand jobs, although rail transportation is expected to decline as truck transportation grows. The warehousing and storage sector is projected to grow rapidly. Employment in the retail and wholesale trades is expected to increase, driven by growth in population, personal income, and leisure time. Employment in utilities is projected to decrease; despite increased output, employment in electric power generation, transmission, and distribution and natural gas distribution is expected to decline due to improved technology that increases worker productivity. However, employment in water, sewage, and other systems is expected to increase, because water treatment and waste disposal are very labor-intensive activities.

- **Financial activities.** Real estate sales and rental and leasing are expected to be the fastest-growing portions of this sector. Finance and insurance are expected to add nearly five hundred thousand jobs. Employment in securities, commodity contracts, and other financial investments and related activities is expected to grow as a result of the increased number of baby boomers in their peak savings years, the growth of tax-favorable retirement plans, and the globalization of the securities markets. Insurance carriers and related activities are expected to add 215,000 jobs.

- **Government.** By 2014, government employment, including that in public education and hospitals, is expected to increase by 10 percent. Growth in this area will be fueled by increases in state and local educational services and the shift of responsibilities from the federal government to state and local governments. Local government educational services are projected to add nearly eight hundred thousand jobs. State government educational services are projected to add more than four hundred thousand jobs. Federal government employment, including the postal service, is expected to increase by only 1.6 percent as the federal government continues to contract out many government jobs to private companies.

- **Other services.** The fastest-growing industry will be automotive repair and maintenance, followed by personal-care services.

Imagination Is a Plus

Perhaps you'll choose a business because you perceive a need for it in your neighborhood or area, or perhaps you'll use your imagination to think up a new enterprise. That is the real advantage of this industry—the opportunity to start something new for fun and profit.

Some of the businesses you'll read about in this book fit into standard categories, such as restaurants and cleaning services. Others are a bit more innovative, such as turning a collecting hobby into a business and offering morale-boosting services to major corporations. So don't be confined by what already exists. Let your imagination soar, be as creative as you can be, and you might come up with a winning idea for a successful new service business that will have customers flooding your website and filling your voice mail with requests for appointments!

Organization of This Book

The first eight chapters present questions relating to you, your abilities, and personal preferences that you should consider before you venture into a business of your own. These are really nuts-and-bolts topics. They provide valuable information about business and finance for anyone considering a business career, whether as an independent businessperson or as a paid employee.

Chapters 9 through 15 outline various types of service businesses that you might consider. They will introduce you to several independent businesspeople who, like you, also once dreamed of becoming entrepreneurs and forged ahead to achieve success. As you read these chapters, you might want to try to visualize how you can utilize your personality, interests, and talents in each of these businesses.

Acknowledgment

The author wishes to thank Josephine Scanlon for her assistance in preparing this revision.

1

SERVICE BUSINESS TRADE-OFFS

THE STATE OF the economy is an important topic. Not a day passes without news reports on factors that affect it; entire television programs are devoted to the subject. If you are planning to start your own business, it's quite possible that you are well aware of the current economic situation and perhaps have even been affected by it yourself.

During the last two decades of the twentieth century, more workers in the United States found themselves unemployed than at any other time, except during the depression of the 1930s. During those years, waves of corporate mergers continued to change the face of business. When one company absorbed another, management often decided that the combined workforce was unnecessary. The surviving company cut all costs to help pay for the merger as well as make the maximum profit.

As a result of mergers and downsizing, many workers no longer felt secure in their jobs as they watched longtime associates fired, sometimes with little notice. As new managements took over, many dismissals seemed unnecessary and cruel. As a result, employee loyalty faltered and morale slipped. This can hurt any company, but it became especially serious for some businesses in the transportation and automobile industries, where safety is an enormous issue and a dissatisfied employee might inadvertently contribute to safety problems. Unhappiness at work can have a negative impact on a company's profit margin.

In light of all this, many people idealize self-employment, but whether they can take the leap to becoming entrepreneurs themselves depends on many factors such as age, geographical location, type of business and potential market for its services, ability to raise the necessary capital, and knowledge of how to operate a business.

Many service businesses offer opportunities both to young people who are just graduating from high school or college and those who already have several years of working experience. Before you give serious thought to whether there might be a service business in your career future, let's briefly explore the advantages and disadvantages of such an activity.

Advantages

There are several advantages to owning a service business. Consider the following as you think about embarking on such a career.

- You are your own boss; you may plan and run the business as you wish without obtaining approval from anyone.
- You can come and go freely.
- You can have the satisfaction of building your own establishment.

- You can keep the profits and reinvest them in the business or you can invest them elsewhere, whichever you decide is best.
- You may hire relatives and friends if you think they are qualified.
- You can give or sell the business to whomever you deem best suited to continue it when you retire or die.

Disadvantages

Of course, where there are advantages there will also be disadvantages. Think carefully about the following points before moving forward with your idea.

- You are solely responsible for the company's well-being and future.
- You must raise the necessary capital to start your enterprise and, if you borrow money, be responsible for meeting all interest and other debt obligations.
- You must be sure to keep careful financial and operating records, bearing in mind the many local, state, provincial, and federal reports (including income tax) that you may have to file.
- You are free to come and go but only if you have someone to cover for you or the nature of the business permits you to be away from it. You may find yourself more tied down than you ever imagined.
- You are responsible for maintaining employee morale, customer satisfaction, and profitable operation that will enable you to meet all obligations.

- You must be ready to assume responsibility for a regular payroll. This is vital to your employees, who depend on their checks for supporting themselves and their families.
- You are *it* in every sense of the word!

After you have given careful thought and consideration to the above, you still must decide whether you are the type of individual who can logically become an entrepreneur with all the ramifications this role entails.

2

IS A SERVICE BUSINESS RIGHT FOR YOU?

No ONE KNOWS you better than you know yourself. And though that may seem perfectly obvious, it's a fact that many of us overlook. You are the only one who knows which kinds of books you like to read, what games or sports you prefer, how you like to spend your free time, what you think is important in life, and what you'd really like to do for a living. But you may be a bit hesitant to reveal your inner thoughts because they may vary from what you think your parents or friends believe in or because your ideas don't conform to what you may think is "normal" or expected.

Fortunately, today's high school and college students are more likely to be encouraged to pursue their career goals than were past generations. Boys are no longer automatically expected to continue their father's line of work—unless they want to. And girls aren't relegated to secretarial jobs and raising families. There are many options available today, and many offer the opportunity to virtually create your own career rather than follow a prescribed path. Most schools offer vocational guidance, and libraries and the Internet offer an abundance of resources that can help you make an informed and intelligent career choice.

Importance of Personality

We've all come across a local merchant or business owner whose personality leaves something to be desired. The proprietor of the local mini-mart may complain about the customers, finding fault with young people who leave items on the shelves in disarray and expressing annoyance at customers who mess up the neatly stacked newspapers when making their selections. He may be visibly irritable when accepting a delivery or when asked to make change for a large bill. He might even chase away children who take too long deciding which treats to buy.

So, if the local store owner is such a mean guy, why do we patronize his business? Because the market on the next block always looks dirty, doesn't carry the latest magazines and newspapers, and often sells stale food. Even though the owner is a nicer person, the quality of her merchandise sends us back to the unfriendly proprietor around the corner. But if the kindly store owner cleaned up her shop and took better care of her business, our cranky merchant would have some competition that might make him reevaluate his surly attitude.

Everyone has an occasional bad day, but to work in a service business, you have to be outwardly positive despite that bad mood. You can't count on the competition offering substandard service to keep customers putting up with your attitude. If you start a service business and find that your attitude toward customers is regularly unfriendly or antagonistic, or that you simply can't leave a bad mood at home, you are probably in the wrong occupation.

Questions to Consider

Here are some questions to think about before starting. Don't be tempted to skim over them quickly, because unless you're prepared to spend considerable time really thinking about most of these questions and discussing them with people who know you well, you may discover some day that you made a terrible mistake.

- **Personal goals.** What do I want to do with my life? Where does my family fit into these goals? Would a service business interfere with my family or personal life?
- **Financial goals.** Is my goal to become rich or do I want to make enough money to live comfortably? Is it likely that the business I am considering can enable me to achieve my financial goal? Would I be good at managing money?
- **Business goals.** What do I hope to achieve in my business? Is my goal financial reward or personal satisfaction? Do I want to operate a small one- or two-man business or do I hope to develop a large organization?
- **Interests.** What interests me most? Would I prefer working with others or working by myself? Will I be better at selling a service or a product? Should I consider performing a service, manufacturing a product, or some other aspect of business?
- **Working preferences.** Would I prefer to work indoors or outdoors? Will I be more comfortable in an urban area, in the suburbs, or in a rural environment? Do I want to move to a new location or stay in my hometown?

Chances are you'll want to start your business in your hometown where you know the most people, are familiar with the community, and could establish the best banking connections. However, if you know that you will be happier living elsewhere, now is the time to make that move before you put down your business and personal roots and later find it difficult to move. It would also be wise to consider whether you will be happier working indoors or outdoors before making a business commitment. For example, although you might like the financial security offered by working as a public stenographer, be sure to consider all the aspects of the job. Will you be comfortable working in an office, spending all day using the necessary equipment to do the job? Practice sitting in an office chair for several hours to see how it feels. If you find yourself daydreaming about working in your garden, you might want to consider a career that will take you outdoors for most of the time.

Many people are happiest working by themselves, preferring not to meet the public or deal with customers. Others are happiest when they are interacting with the public, selling a service or managing a business such as a home cleaning service, laundry, or a restaurant. How you relate to people is an important consideration in choosing a service business.

• **Personality.** How would I rate myself on important personal qualities? Am I friendly and optimistic? Do I have the perseverance and self-confidence to stay with a project? Is my sense of humor sufficient to allow me to interact successfully with others and laugh at my own mistakes? Do I take pride in my work and exude an air of neatness and dependability? Am I willing to learn, both from others and from my own experience? Can I turn criticism into something constructive that might help me improve myself and my business? Can I accept setbacks or problems without becoming discouraged? Can I avoid unnecessary worry and control my emotions and temper if things don't go my way?

Be honest in answering these questions because they address essential assets for anyone in a service business. If you suspect that you could stand improvement in any of these areas, ask yourself whether you could do this. It might be helpful to have two or three friends rate you on each area. You might be surprised at what you will learn, and it could be very beneficial.

• **Impression.** Do I make a positive impression on others? If not, how can I work to improve this? Do I inspire confidence or do I make others feel uneasy?

What friends and business associates think about the impression you make on others is meaningful and helpful. Again, it's wise to seek opinions from people who will give you an honest appraisal.

• **Qualifications.** What business experience and training have I had that would prepare me for the enterprise I would like to start? Have I obtained any basic management experience or knowledge that will be important when I start my own business? How well do I manage my personal and family finances? Do I have any special or unusual talents or skills that might be useful in some type of business that I have not considered? Do I have leadership qualities?

Many new enterprises fail because, unfortunately, people often open businesses for which they have little or no training or experience. But don't be discouraged if you lack the background and skills needed for a particular activity. Find a job in that field, obtain actual working experience, and when you feel ready to go out on your own you will certainly be far better prepared to run your own service.

• **Working habits.** Can I discipline myself to work long hours if necessary? Would I be unhappy spending more than eight hours a day in my business? Do I have what it takes to stay with a job as long as necessary, even though it may inconvenience me or my family? Am I a hard worker?

• **Family reaction.** Will my family understand and support my idea? Will they cut back expenses and make sacrifices if necessary and perhaps help me with the business? Would a business of my own disrupt educational, vacation, or other family plans? Will running the business from home cause any inconvenience?

As you consider these questions, keep in mind that you are about to make one of the most important choices of your life. Avoid the temptation of rushing to reach a decision. Be sure to take your family into your confidence, discuss everything with them, and be ready to listen to their suggestions and criticisms. They know you very well and their opinions deserve to be heard.

Can You Afford Your Own Business?

Starting your own business calls for experience, know-how, courage—and cash! Suddenly there is no income, and you are financially dependent on those first customers who patronize your new service. Before your grand opening, however, there will be expenses for supplies, equipment, tools, perhaps a vehicle, or whatever your particular enterprise requires. You'll need sufficient funds to cover those initial capital needs.

Your new business isn't the only financial consideration. Remember that you will also have to finance your normal living expenses during those first weeks and months when you're introducing your service and building up patronage. You may be lucky and enjoy a fine cash flow right from the start, but this is something you should never count on.

Consider the following questions in relation to your financial situation and your plans for the business:

- Have you thought of the advantages and disadvantages of buying an existing service business?
- Do you know how much money it costs a month for all your household, personal, and family expenses?
- Have you estimated how much money you will have to invest in the business?
- Have you made a conservative forecast of income and expenses for your service and determined how much profit you will earn?
- Will your savings be sufficient, or can you obtain enough money from various sources to cover expected capital needs and provide for living expenses for some time to come?
- Do you have other financial resources for emergencies?

You will find that most of these questions cannot be answered easily. In Chapter 6 there is useful information about how to make your financial plans, but even at this early stage you should have a fairly good idea of what it will take to start your business, how much you can expect to make, and what your expenses will be.

Is There a Need for Your Service Business?

You have decided that you have the necessary qualifications, personality, and financial ability to undertake the service business that you are eager to start. One final important question remains: is there a need for your service?

Have you done enough research to make certain that the public either requires (as in the case of a dry cleaning business) or desires (as in the case of a home catering business) your service? If there is no similar business in the town or neighborhood where you propose to operate, are you likely to attract enough customers? Are the residents ready for and able to support the service you will offer? Some communities are simply not sophisticated enough to accept a service that is highly successful in another town. People's social and economic backgrounds, as well as local customs, often dictate purchasing habits, preferences, and prejudices, and it may prove difficult, if not impossible, to overcome them.

Equally important is the question of whether the community can afford your service, even though it might want to use it. If a large number of people are retired and living on small pensions or Social Security, and the balance of the population is made up of low- or middle-income workers with large families, your chance of introducing a luxury or nonessential service is doomed to failure before you begin. Again and again an entrepreneur starts a business for which there is no market, a mistake that can be avoided by taking the time beforehand to find out if the public could afford it.

So, to a large degree, the market determines your success or failure. At this point it's a good idea to consider what prospects there may be for growth. You want your business to increase, but if you locate in an area that people are leaving or where there is a stagnant population, your future could be uncertain.

During the last two decades, the country has seen drastic changes in the market and economy as industries relocated, factories closed, wages were cut, and workforces were reduced, creating economic havoc in many cities and towns. You don't want to be caught in such a situation by plant closings or any other adverse economic events. Make certain that the area you plan to operate in is not likely to be affected by economic change.

In addition to local problems, you should think carefully about whether your proposed business would be able to survive larger economic fluctuations such as inflation and recession. Businesses offering luxury or nonessential services are bound to suffer in times of depression, unless customers are wealthy enough not to be affected by general economic adversity.

Another important factor to consider is whether your customers will be one-time users or repeat users. Obviously, a kitchen remodeling service cannot expect frequent repeat business, even from satisfied customers. Conversely, a chimney-cleaning service should find repeat customers in an area where wood-burning stoves and fireplaces are in common use. If your service caters only to onetime customers, will you have a large enough area and potential market to ensure business for many years? Have you considered the competition? If so, is there already so much competition as to make it risky for you to enter the market, too, or is there enough business for all to share and still make a profit? On the other hand, perhaps there is need for another service that will be superior to others already in operation. By all means study your potential competitors and learn their strong and weak points. List the ways your business will differ from theirs as well as how your service will be better or inferior. Finally, put yourself in the position of a customer and ask yourself why someone would patronize your service rather than that of another.

You will have less time-consuming investigation to do if no one else is operating the same service you propose to offer, but the questions regarding size of the market and acceptance of your service still apply. That is why, in addition to your own careful consideration of the prospects for success, you should talk with a number of people who are in a position to advise you.

Ask for Advice

In addition to learning how your family feels about your service business ideas, it's a very good idea to seek guidance from two or three people who you think might be able to advise you. Impartial advice is always helpful; you don't have to follow it, but you may find that it proves beneficial, raises questions that hadn't occurred to you, and might even steer you in an entirely different and better direction.

Try to talk with small business operators who are in a line similar to the one you are contemplating. Tell them about your plans and ask whether they think your business idea is a good one, whether they foresee any pitfalls, whether they can offer any suggestions, and whether they can recommend any other people you should talk to or resources you should consult.

You should also consider talking with a loan officer at your bank. These professionals are experienced in judging whether you are qualified for such an undertaking and also whether you are taking a sensible business risk. Before they lend money, loan officers must know everything about you and the business you propose to undertake. Although you won't be requesting funds at this point, you may need to borrow money later, and it's a good idea to know in advance whether a banker would consider your loan application favorably. If the loan officer indicates there is a good possibility of lending you money, you can assume that your prospects are good.

If you don't have any friends in business you feel free to question, talk with the owner of a store where you shop, a real estate broker, the person who runs the local hardware store, or the owner of a hotel, motel, or restaurant in town. Established businesspeople are usually glad to share their knowledge and experience. It is flattering to be sought out for advice, so don't hesitate to ask for it.

There are some very helpful resources available that offer a variety of information about starting your own business. America's Website for Education and Development offers online courses as well as articles on different aspects of owning a business. Visit www.awed.org for information.

An excellent source of information is the U.S. Small Business Administration (www.sba.gov). The SBA website provides resources for planning and managing your business, services for financial assistance and training, tools for marketing and research, and local resources. The administration also sponsors SCORE (Service Corps of Retired Executives), a program staffed by thousands of volunteer retired or active businesspeople who are specialists in various fields. They advise small businesses like the one you plan, and there is no charge for their services.

The SBA also sponsors the Office of Women's Business Ownership, which maintains a network of women's business owner representatives in every SBA district office, more than eighty women's business centers, more than 160 mentoring roundtables, and several women-owned venture capital companies. There are programs to help women put together successful loan packages or break into the federal procurement and export markets, as well as loan guaranty programs to help those who cannot get lending through conventional channels to finance their businesses. The Online Women's Business Center helps women start and build successful businesses with training, advice, and counseling via the Internet.

Industry Canada sponsors Strategis, a service for businesses and consumers. The website, http://strategis.ic.gc.ca, provides information on various aspects of business. The Business Start-Up Assistant, organized by topic and province, provides information on market research, business name and structure, preparing a business plan, financing, taxation, hiring employees, and doing business on the Internet.

If there is a chamber of commerce or board of trade in your area, see the executive director and get an opinion of your project. You may also be able to get names of businesspeople who may be helpful. Most chambers of commerce maintain websites; you can check online for member businesses that you think would be a good place to start.

Another source of information may be the trade association for the service in which you are interested. Consult *Gale's Encyclopedia of Associations*, which you will find at most large public or university libraries.

Numerous books are also listed in the Suggested Reading at the end of the book.

Your Final Decision

After you have completed your investigations and had your interviews, you should be ready to make that final decision—yes or no. You alone must determine whether you should go into business for yourself and whether your choice of a service is the correct one. If you have reservations, are uncertain, fearful, or not entirely sold on the idea, it's best to postpone any further action. Continue in your present occupation or find a job in or related to the service area that interests you. This could be a very good way of accumulating valuable experience for the future.

On the other hand, if you're absolutely sure that you are an entrepreneur at heart, that you have what it takes and will be successful, then move ahead with your business plans.

3

GETTING READY

You NOW KNOW the questions you should consider carefully before you start your own service business. If you are satisfied that the advantages outweigh the disadvantages and that you could handle any disadvantages that might occur, then you are most likely enthusiastic about embarking on your career. In other words, you firmly believe that you are suited to start and operate a service in some niche of this industry, and that one way or another you will be able to obtain the experience and necessary financial backing you'll need before announcing plans for the grand opening.

It's important to be practical and avoid becoming impatient—an inexperienced businessperson can't expect to become an entrepreneur overnight. However, if you have experience and capital, you should be able to start fairly quickly once you've found a site for the business, done the necessary marketing survey, and arranged adequate financing. Whatever your status, beware of rushing in without being certain that your plan is sensible and that you have sufficient financial backing. You don't want to become just another business statistic that closes its doors within five or fewer years, five years being considered by many as the average period needed to get a business on a firm financial footing.

Questions to Consider

To be successful, you'll need a good understanding of accounting, marketing, personnel management, promotion, and administration, as well as a thorough knowledge of the business you are about to enter. With this in mind, it will be tremendously helpful if you research the following areas and can answer each question sensibly.

- **Does the industry have a trade association?** Trade associations can be invaluable sources of statistics, studies, and information about the industry. Membership benefits often include newsletters, annual conventions, and educational opportunities. Many associations offer discounted memberships for students. For a list of trade associations consult the *Encyclopedia of Associations*, a regularly updated publication available in your library.
- **Have you read any of the principal industry periodicals or books?** Copies of journals may be available in your library, or the reference librarian may be able to help you locate them. Consult the *Gale Directory of Publications and Broadcast Media*, an annual directory. Search the Internet for publications of interest.
- **What are the growth prospects for the industry?** Check the trade journals and projections made by the U.S. Bureau of Labor Statistics (www.bls.gov) to learn about the outlook for the next few years.
- **How have past economic downturns affected the industry?** Trade associations and government information can be helpful here

as well. Carefully consider to what extent the industry has been affected by the economy in the past, and try to determine whether it can sustain future economic shifts.

• **Who are your principal competitors, especially in your local area if you are starting a service in your hometown?** Consult your chamber of commerce to see how many similar businesses are already in existence.

• **What are the most effective ways to market your new service?** Think about all of the advertising you've seen for similar businesses and try to come up with a fresher, newer campaign. Consult some of the books listed in the Suggested Reading at the end of this book for marketing ideas.

• **What, if any, new businesses or technical changes pose future threats to your service business?** For example, companies that sold "smoke-eaters," machines designed to reduce the effect of cigarette smoke in public places, lost most of their business in the last decade due to the steadily increasing number of restaurants and bars that ban smoking.

For answers to the above questions, consult sources such as the industry's trade association, the *Reader's Guide to Periodical Literature, Industrial Arts Index*, your chamber of commerce, and any other sources your librarian may suggest. Search the Internet as well for even more sources of information.

Obtain Business Experience

One factor that is essential to your new endeavor is the amount of experience you bring to it. If you are serious about starting a service business, there are many options to consider as possible sources of valuable experience.

If You Are Working

If you are currently working and must wait before you can open your own service business, consider starting a business that you can operate during evenings and weekends. Unless moonlighting is impractical because your employer forbids it or you couldn't fit it into your schedule, it is an excellent way to obtain valuable experience in operating your own business. Just as important, it's a way to earn extra money—money that might help speed up the day when you will be your own full-time boss.

Ideally, you may be able to moonlight in the service business that you hope to open. However, if this isn't the case, you can look to your other interests and skills for some business ideas.

If You Are in School

If you are still in high school or college, you might be able to start a business of your own during the summer or on weekends. This would give you welcome extra cash, experience in owning and running your own enterprise, and perhaps some idea of what you might want to do when the time comes to be on your own.

Here are some ideas for businesses you can start and operate part-time whether you are working or in school, after classes and on weekends, as well as during summer vacations. Be sure the one you choose will find a ready number of customers in your town and that the competition is not so intense you won't be able to obtain a share of business for yourself.

Accounting for small businesses
Appliance repair

Automobile detailing
Babysitting
Bartending
Carpentry
Catering
Cleaning service
Computer assistance/repair
Deejay/emcee
Dressmaking/alterations
Driving instructor
Electrical repair
Electronics repair/service
Hairstylist
Home repair
House sitting
Income tax preparation
Interior design/decorating
Laundry services
Lawn and garden services
Manicurist
Painting
Party planning
Personal chef
Personal shopper
Pet care/sitting
Photography
Plumbing
Real estate sales
Résumé preparation

Secretarial service
Sewing/mending
Tutor

Be sure to review the various service businesses covered in Chapters 9 through 15, too. One of them might provide an idea for part-time work while you gain experience. The books listed in the Suggested Reading at the end of this volume might also be a good starting point.

In addition to working part-time, you might be able to fit in a course or two at a local vocational/technical school, adult education program, or community college.

Take Appropriate Academic Courses

If you are in high school or college, you may have the opportunity to take business-related courses that will prove worthwhile regardless of what you do after graduation. If your schedule can accommodate it, take classes in bookkeeping or accounting, typing, business English, and computers. College offers a wide variety of economics and business courses, which can be taken as electives in a liberal arts program, giving you a broad educational base.

Don't forget about English courses! Good grammar and spelling are very important in a successful business. Unfortunately, poor grammar and sloppy speech is often interpreted as a sign of carelessness or ignorance, an impression you don't want to make on your customers. If you suspect that your grammar needs work, ask a friend who has a good command of the language to let you know when you make mistakes. Then by concentrating on these, you can gradually train yourself to avoid errors.

Become Well Informed

Read widely and be as well informed as possible. Your reading should include a daily newspaper, a national news magazine, a general business periodical, and a magazine devoted to the service area that interests you, or one aimed at entrepreneurs like yourself. Ideas come from reading, and if you are going to operate your own business, you should have an inquiring and well-informed mind. Be aware that in many service businesses, you may have frequent and extensive interactions with clients. In these situations, the ability to maintain an interesting conversation or to comment intelligently on current affairs is always beneficial. Although you may not think that what you are reading is useful to your business plans, you can never tell when something may spark an idea.

Pay attention to other businesses that you deal with. Notice how you are received as a customer or client, whether the employees are prompt and courteous in attending to you, and whether they seem eager to serve you. Do the employees know their business? Is the service all you expect? If the answers to these questions are "no," remember that it's possible that the employees haven't been properly trained but just hired and expected to do the job. This is sometimes the case in stores, where workers are seen talking on their cell phones or conversing together while customers wait for attention. Think about how you would prevent these situations. On the other hand, if the service is excellent, think about how the owner accomplished this.

Try to make it a habit to mentally review all of your business transactions, regardless of whether they are with a service enterprise. By observing and recording the strengths and weaknesses of other businesses, you'll build up helpful background information to which you can refer when you are ready to open your own business.

Don't risk forgetting any good ideas you may have. Carry a small notebook and pen with you at all times, or send yourself an e-mail or voice message as a reminder of any ideas that occur throughout your day. These reminders will also come in handy when you see something you think might be useful in your business or worth investigating.

A Final Word

If the service business you have chosen is right for you, you can make it succeed. Nothing is more satisfying to someone who wants to be an independent entrepreneur than to become just that. Remember that the road to independence demands study, hard work, and perseverance, so experience and knowledge of your chosen business are essential to your success.

Taking that first step into the unknown isn't easy, but if it leads to what you want, you can do it. Once you're on your own, you are not necessarily all alone. Remember, the Service Corps of Retired Executives (SCORE); the Small Business Administration (SBA); Strategis, Canada's business and consumer site on the Net; your local bank; and fellow businesspeople are all useful allies, too. College or university professors of business administration may be available for consultation. Don't forget trade associations as sources of advice and encouragement. Most important, you will have your own common sense and business know-how to help solve problems.

But first you must face a few more important questions relating to the location and operation of your new business, which will be covered in the next chapters.

4

Important Decisions to Make

Most of us have no idea how local businesses, law firms, large manufacturers, airlines, hotels, or other establishments are organized. There is no need for the average person to know, and schools devote little or no time to the subject, except in certain economics courses. However, now that you are considering opening your own service business, you've moved out of the ranks of the average person and into the realm of the businessperson—and now there is a reason for you to understand how business works.

Types of Business Organizations

One of your big decisions will be determining the official organization of your business.

There are four kinds of business organizations—a sole proprietorship, a partnership of two or more individuals, a stock corporation, and a limited liability company—and it's important to know which is right for your situation.

the four forms of business organization has its advan-
disadvantages. You should carefully consider all of these
e deciding what is best for your company.

Sole Proprietorship

The sole proprietorship is the least complicated. You give your business a name and it becomes your company. You may have to register the company name with the town clerk, county clerk, or
secretary of state, depending on your state or provincial law, but
other than that requirement, you probably need only file your usual
federal, state, and local income tax reports.

Advantages and Disadvantages

The advantages are that a proprietorship is easy to organize, offers
tax advantages, and may require little or no capital to start. In addition, you are the boss and the profits are yours to keep.

The disadvantages include possible difficulty obtaining bank
loans and the possibility of being personally sued and losing everything that you own.

Partnership

Professionals who wish to practice together can form a partnership.
It's important to have a lawyer draw up a partnership agreement
that specifies the various points agreed upon by the partners regarding the operation of the business, the responsibilities of each, the
division of profits, and the respective liability for losses. Too often
friends enter into a partnership believing that the strength of their
relationship can withstand any potential problems. Unfortunately,

friendships often dissolve along with businesses when things don't go as planned.

Advantages and Disadvantages

A partnership is generally easy to organize and allows broader management possibilities than a proprietorship; there are also certain tax advantages.

Disadvantages include possible difficulty securing loans and the potential difficulties that may arise from having two or more bosses. As with a proprietorship, the owners may be sued.

Stock Corporation

The stock corporation (or S-corporation) is an impersonal entity without a face or a heart. Articles of incorporation list the purposes of the new corporation, the types of businesses in which it may engage, and the form of organization. A board of directors, usually a minimum of three, may be provided to give overall direction to the company. Its members, in turn, name the officers who run the business.

The officers usually consist of a president, vice president, treasurer, and secretary, but the same individual may hold more than one office. If you organize a stock corporation, you might sell shares of stock to yourself, members of your family, and a few friends. These would become the stockholders and elect the directors—who might be themselves. They would then elect the officers, again perhaps themselves.

Although this may seem illogical, it does mean that if the corporation is sued, you are not personally liable unless it is proven that you have acted in a criminal or otherwise illegal manner.

If you hope to raise money from friends or others for your new service, this is probably the best form of organization because you can sell the backers shares of stock. Depending on how many shares they purchase, they might control the company, which would help them protect their investment.

This really isn't as complicated as it sounds, and hundreds of thousands of small corporations are organized for every conceivable reason. You aren't obligated to have a board of directors or to sell stock, but these are options that you might want to consider.

Corporations, though, must file all kinds of tax returns—city, state, and federal—and this is often a compelling reason for not incorporating. You can certainly file the papers of incorporation yourself, but many new business owners choose to have an attorney or certified public accountant handle this transaction.

Advantages and Disadvantages

The advantages of a stock corporation include the ability to easily transfer ownership and maintain the life of the company in the event of the death of a director, officer, or stockholder. It also may be easier to secure financing for a corporation than for the other two types of organization. Personal liability of officers and directors is limited in the event of a lawsuit.

On the negative side, a corporation may be costly to organize and is regulated by state law. Taxes must be carefully attended to and detailed records maintained.

Limited Liability Company

The limited liability company (LLC) is a relatively new form of business organization that combines the advantages of the other three forms. An LLC is a separate legal entity, similar to a corporation, which is also treated as a partnership for tax purposes. As with a sole proprietorship, it isn't necessary to keep minutes, hold meetings, or make corporate resolutions.

Owners of an LLC are called *members*. In most localities, members may include individuals, corporations, other LLCs, and foreign entities. There is no maximum number of members. Most states also permit single-member LLCs, which are those having only one owner.

Advantages and Disadvantages

As with a corporation, the owners of an LLC are protected against personal liability in the event of legal action against the company. It is also generally fairly easy to secure financing.

On the other hand, as a member of an LLC, you are not allowed to pay yourself wages, and the managing member's share of the company's bottom-line profit is considered earned income and, therefore, is subject to self-employment tax.

In light of all these advantages and disadvantages, your best plan is to consult an attorney for help in deciding which type of business organization is best for you.

Choose a Location

Two couples decided to buy motels in Pennsylvania's Pocono Mountains. One couple not only did a market survey but also carefully researched the location. They studied road maps and measured distances from principal cities in the central and northeast states to see where most travelers would be by nightfall. Then they visited the three areas indicated and, by driving around and carefully observing where motels hung up the most "No Vacancy" signs, determined the best location. Next they undertook their market research and, satisfied with what they learned, a year later bought an attractive motel with fifteen units. It proved a successful business.

The other couple visited a real estate office in a resort town, learned of several motels that were for sale, and bought what they considered the most attractive and least expensive. A few weeks after they had taken possession, they learned that a new bypass would be coming through the area, taking all the traffic away from the road where the motel was located. They were stuck with their property, as it was highly unlikely that they would be able to find another buyer.

It may seem that chances are good that this won't happen to you, but road patterns do shift and neighborhoods can change. Urban renewal projects can wipe out many blocks of buildings, and new shopping centers often siphon off business from older, established downtown areas. It's impossible to know when the bulldozers will start a new shopping mall, creating hardships for existing merchants and businesses. The best you can do is to check with the city or town department that issues building permits and learn what projects have received a green light for development or are in the planning stages.

Location is all-important for some businesses. A restaurant, self-service laundry, motel, service station, or dry-cleaning establishment must be in a busy neighborhood with a steady traffic of people who need the services. On the other hand, if your service is cleaning, appliance repair, or another service in which you go to the customers' homes, it may not matter where your office or base is located. All you need is a telephone number and address so people can find you.

Assuming that your business must be where the action is, you may face the problem of high demand causing high rents. You might be able to locate just off a busy thoroughfare and save money without hurting your business potential. You might also take over an existing lease on a store or building at a moderate rate, or perhaps share space with a business that would welcome you as a means of reducing its overhead. If you can't or don't want to operate your business from home, a low-rental area might offer advantages.

Is a Home Office Right for You?

Operating a business from home offers certain pluses and some minuses that you should consider. Here are some advantages:

- You will enjoy the convenience of rolling out of bed on a snowy morning and being just a few feet from your office.
- You will have the opportunity to work longer hours without having to commute.
- You will save money by avoiding office overhead and taking a tax deduction for use of space within your home.
- You will be able to call on family members to help, especially when you are rushed or unable to handle large jobs by yourself.

The drawbacks are not always as evident to the uninitiated as the advantages, but making a living within the home can be hard on the family:

- Resentment can grow as the business dominates family life and activities.
- The day-to-day demands of the enterprise may gradually eliminate what had always been regular and enjoyable recreational, social, and religious activities.

- There is a temptation for the head of the business to spend too much time working, to the neglect of the family's other needs.
- Business-related telephone calls can become an annoying intrusion at all times of the day and evening.
- The need for customers and others to visit on business can destroy the privacy of the home.
- There is no excuse for not getting the work done. That same snowy morning that would once have meant a day off is no longer a valid reason for not working.

Working from home isn't for everyone; many people need to separate business from home to be most productive and not disrupt family life. On the other hand, some people find maintaining a home office to be an excellent way of getting their work done while still having time for family. This is often the case for single parents or women who want to work while still being available to their children.

Office Supplies and Equipment

Whether you set up your office at home or in a new space, this is one area where it pays to economize—but not too much! Starting your new business is exciting, and it's understandable that you'll want a modern, well-equipped office, one that will please you and impress your customers. This is fine if you have enough capital to splurge on expensive equipment, but it is possible to create a businesslike office with a desk, chairs, filing cabinets, and other furniture purchased at a secondhand office supply house or at a used household furniture store, which can save you a great deal of money.

Before you buy any equipment, look through the house and ask friends to see if they have anything they'd like to donate to your worthy cause. You might be surprised at how a little imagination can transform a spare table into a functional credenza for your working files.

Whatever your business venture is, you'll need a computer. You will have to print estimates and invoices, prepare correspondence, and possibly maintain a website. If you shop carefully, you should be able to find one that meets your needs without breaking your budget. But you might be able to save money on the peripherals to go with that new computer. Rather than buying a printer, a fax machine, and an answering machine, you should consider investing in a multipurpose unit that combines all three functions. Some also function as scanners and allow you to print from your digital camera.

Shopping at the big-box office stores is usually a good way to save money. Staples and Office Depot are two large chains that carry everything from paper clips to office furniture to electronics to cleaning supplies. They also have websites that let you compare prices and shop online.

Your telephone line is an extremely important part of your business. If you operate the business out of your home, you can use your existing telephone number; however, if you can afford a second line, it's a very good idea to have one installed. This is especially important for sending and receiving faxes. There are many different telephone plans available, so you should consider the options carefully before making a decision. Voice-over IP technology allows companies to provide less-expensive service than the big telephone companies, but the latter offer various business plans. You might also consider a plan that gives you a discounted rate on combined telephone and Internet service.

You most likely have a cell phone, which can also play an important role in your business, especially if you will travel to clients to deliver your service. A cell phone is a great way to avoid lost time if you or the client must cancel an appointment.

Accounting System

You've already read that too many businesses fail because of inadequate record keeping. Although you don't have to be a certified public accountant (CPA) to stay abreast of your finances, even if you know a little about bookkeeping, it would still be a good idea for you to contact an accountant or CPA to set up your books and show you how to keep them. Depending on how complicated your business records will be, it might pay to have the work done for you, in which case you would furnish information about all your transactions to the accountant, who would post the books.

You should also consider investing in an accounting software program. These can be expensive, perhaps $300 or $400, but most small business owners wouldn't be without one. There are programs specifically designed for most industries, which give you custom-made estimates, invoices, timesheets, and bill payment options. If you keep excellent records in your software program, you can download the data for your accountant's review rather than submitting bundles of bank statements and receipts.

Administrative Assistance

Administrative services can be expensive. Fortunately, with a cell phone and an answering machine you can access remotely, you shouldn't need someone to answer the phone. But you might be all thumbs around a keyboard. If you can type, be your own secretary at first. If you can't, you might enlist the services of someone who can help you. Some suggested sources are:

- A professional typing/secretarial service listed in the yellow pages or classified ads of your newspaper
- A friend or acquaintance who has a small business and might welcome sharing the services of an administrative assistant
- A local student who is taking a commercial course and would be glad to work for experience and a little cash (contact the teacher in charge of the commercial department or the guidance counselor at the school)
- A family member or friend who might be willing to help out until you are better established, perhaps for a reasonable wage

If your business requires full-time office staff, investigate the possibility of hiring an older or retired person who wants to keep busy and supplement Social Security income. Bear in mind that such a person is mature and may have experience that will be valuable to your business. You can inquire at churches, senior citizen centers, and other organizations for the names of people who might be interested in such work, or try the classified section of your newspaper.

Professional Assistance

As already suggested, you may want to have a lawyer draw up a partnership agreement or incorporation papers. There may also be other subjects on which you'll want to seek legal advice. An attorney with broad knowledge and experience in handling a wide variety of business situations can be both a counselor and sounding board. It's also smart to have a lawyer who knows you and your service in the event that some unexpected legal crisis should arise that calls for immediate action or defense.

What's the best way to find a good lawyer? Although you can find one listed in the yellow pages, the best way to select an attorney is to ask the businesspeople you deal with or friends who are in business.

5

PROFIT OR LOSS?

WHAT IS THE real purpose of a business? Every business, from a service station to a Fortune 500 company, has one basic purpose. Your local service station supplies gasoline and services automobiles, and United Airlines provides transportation services for customers around the world. So what is it that they have in common? They, and every other type of company, exist to make a profit. That is their real purpose.

Once you have begun your service business, you'll quickly realize that if you don't make money, your business will fail. As you may have guessed from its title, money is the subject of this chapter. It takes capital to start any business, and then it takes hard work, sound planning, and excellent service to make money.

Bottom Line

One of the most overworked phrases in business is *the bottom line*. It refers to the last line of the profit-and-loss statement, the numbers that indicate either gain or loss after you subtract your expenses from your income. This final figure tells whether you have succeeded or failed in your objective.

The goal as the owner of a service business is twofold: to provide service in the specialized area you have selected and to make money. The first goal enables you to attain the second. However, it's important to note that even if you provide the best service in the world, if you mismanage your finances, the bottom line is going to show a red figure—loss. Everything in this chapter is aimed at ensuring that the bottom line of your statements will show positive figures, indicating gain and success.

Now, before you do anything else, find a pencil, some paper, and enough time to do some financial analysis. It shouldn't be difficult, it can be fun, and you will learn some surprising things about yourself, your finances, and what you should expect to earn in your enterprise.

Before you start your business, you must fully review your own financial situation: the minimum income you need to pay the rent or mortgage and buy groceries, how much money you can afford to invest in the business, and how much capital you will require to begin operating. This information is crucial. If you find that at this time you cannot afford to start your business, or that it will not make sufficient money to support you, you should postpone your plans until a financial reassessment shows that the numbers are in your favor.

Keep in mind that the income and expense figures shown throughout this chapter are not intended to suggest the amount of money you should spend or budget. They are not realistic in many geographic areas but are used to illustrate the various steps required in preparing a financial plan for your business.

Six Financial-Planning Steps

You have considered marketing your business, your business idea is feasible, you have the necessary experience or training, and you have some savings or can borrow money to start your business. (Fortunately many service enterprises require little capital, but a few do call for a fair amount of start-up money.) Now you are ready to do your financial planning.

The bottom line of your financial statement will have to equal or exceed the amount of money you need for living expenses, unless you have adequate savings. Profit, which the business makes beyond your living requirements, will be welcome surplus cash, but it may take months or years before you begin depositing extra dollars in the bank. Therefore, you must be exceedingly careful and conservative as you look ahead and draw up your financial projections.

Unfortunately there's no sure way to know what is going to happen. Part of the planning depends on your deciding, guessing, estimating, and forecasting how much your business will earn. You will be forced to make some assumptions, and this is where previous business experience will help because you can draw on your knowledge rather than make wild guesses. If you don't have any prior experience, ask for help from others in the same line of business or from knowledgeable friends.

There are two good reasons for doing a thorough financial forecast: it could be disastrous to start a business without one, and you will need all this information to obtain a loan.

Step 1: Draw Up a Budget

The first step in doing a financial forecast is to draw up a budget for your personal or family living needs. It's important to be realistic about your expenses. Don't overlook any expense item and don't be extravagant either. Allow some money for recreation—you must have a little fun but you don't have to go to the most expensive movies or restaurants. Budget something for emergencies or unforeseen circumstances, such as a broken appliance or emergency auto repair.

The personal budget is an essential part of your financial plan because it shows you how much income your business must make to support you. It is impossible to overemphasize how important it is to know your personal financial needs. Too many people have started a business without taking this step and have found to their dismay that the enterprise could never make enough money to support them adequately.

Following is a monthly budget prepared by Janet Fisher, a single woman who has been trained as a hairstylist, has worked in a beauty salon for two years, and wants to start her own business.

Personal Monthly Budget

Food	$400
Rent	$900
Utilities	$120
Cell phone	$20
Clothing	$140
Car payment	$200
Car insurance	$60
Gasoline	$100
Health insurance	$140
Medical expenses	$80
Life insurance	$40
Recreation	$100

Spending money	$120
Personal gifts	$40
Emergencies	$100
Total	$2,560

The total of Janet's monthly expenses, $2,560, is the figure her hair-dressing business will have to earn per month to meet all of her expenses.

Step 2: Invest in Your Business

Now that you know your monthly expenses, you must determine how much money you have on hand that is available to invest in your business. Even if you have little or no cash, by all means go through this exercise anyway. You may be able to borrow what you need.

This is what Janet set down for her financial situation.

Available Capital

Savings account:	$2,300
Twenty shares of Eureka Industries common stock, market value @ $67 a share:	$1,340
Total:	$3,640

Step 3: List Your Capital Expenditures

Step 3 is to list your anticipated capital expenditures, which are permanent additions or improvements to property. These would include all the equipment, furniture, fixtures, and other items you will need to start your business, as contrasted to supplies like stationery, cleaning materials, or uniforms. Consider what Janet Fisher has to buy for her beauty salon and you'll understand what is meant by capital requirements.

Janet made a list of the minimum equipment she would need to open her salon. She knows where to purchase much of it second-hand, and a friend who is a plumber offered to help her install the sinks and redecorate the space she planned to lease. Her list included the following items:

Item	*Number*
Revolving chairs	2
Chair for dryer	1
Standing dryer	1
Blow dryers	2
Sinks	2
Chairs with arms for the waiting area	3
Full-length mirrors	2
Electric razor	1
Sets of combs	6
Pairs of scissors	6
Desk	1
Desk chair	1
Coat rack	1
Vacuum cleaner	1
Sets of shelves to hold equipment	2
Metal cabinet-type closet	1

In addition to the capital items, Janet listed a number of expenses for supplies: lotions, solutions, rollers, towels, smocks, soaps and other cosmetic items, writing paper, pens, paper clips, stapling machine, account books, desk lamp, and wastepaper basket. None of these items is expensive, but their cost must be anticipated. Janet's total capital and cash requirements total $12,000.

After you have made a list of your anticipated capital and start-up expenses, you know what your cash needs will be to start your enterprise. So far so good, but you still don't know whether the business will earn enough to support you. How are you going to decide this? The answer is simple: by preparing two more estimates—one of income, the other of your operating expenses—and then put them together in a cash position projection.

Step 4: Prepare Your Income Projection

Now it's time to prepare your income projection, the most difficult of all the steps. Without the ability to look into the future, the best you can do is to work out some kind of sensible plan for what you might expect to take in at the cash register.

Janet Fisher knows that working alone she can handle ten customers a day. Since each of the services she plans to offer will carry different fees ($40 for a haircut; $75 for a permanent; $35 for a shampoo, set, and dry; and so forth) she worked out what she thinks would be an average hourly income. This gave her the basic figure she needed: $43.75. This figure represents $350 for an eight-hour day, assuming she works right through from nine until five and serves ten customers who want the least-expensive service she offers. However, being new to the area, Janet realizes that she won't be busy at once and, therefore, estimates that for the first month she will be busy perhaps 25 percent of the time and for the second month 40 percent. If people are pleased with her work and tell their friends about her, perhaps she'll be busy 60 percent of the time for the next four months. Thereafter she should be busy all day. Her arithmetic is quite simple and her projections are reasonable.

Anticipated Income

Average income per day	$350
Average income per week (six days)	$2,100
Average income per month (assume four weeks)	$8,400
First month income (25 percent of $8,400)	$2,100
Second month income (40 percent of $8,400)	$3,360
Third, fourth, fifth, and sixth months income (60 percent of $8,400)	$5,040
Monthly income thereafter	$8,400

Remember, the figures listed are Janet's anticipated gross income; she still must consider the expenses of running the business.

Step 5: Forecast Your Expenses

Step 5 is to prepare your forecast of expenses—what it will cost you each month to operate the business. There will be overhead costs such as rent, telephone, payroll, supplies, insurance, taxes, utilities, interest on borrowed money, and loan payments.

Notice that Janet's list of monthly operating expenses includes two kinds of expenses: those that occur every month, such as utilities and wages; and those that are payable once or twice a year, such as licenses, insurance, property taxes, and dues. So if your insurance costs $2,400 a year, your list of monthly expenses would not show $2,400 but one-twelfth of that amount, or $200, and you would accumulate $200 each month in the bank so as to have the $2,400 when it came due.

Monthly Operating Expenses

Rent	$900
Taxes ($1,200 payable in April)	$100
Supplies	$120
Electricity	$220
Telephone	$100
Heat	$120
License ($240 payable in October)	$20
Insurance ($288 payable in January)	$24
Bank payment	$320
Dues ($144 payable in July)	$12
Total	$1,936

Now we are ready to look at the bottom line of Janet's simplified financial forecasts.

Month 1

Estimated income	$1,257.80
Estimated expenses	$1,936
Gain (or loss)	$(678.20)

Month 2

Estimated income	$2,016
Estimated expenses	$1,936
Gain (or loss)	$80

Months 3, 4, 5, and 6

Estimated income	$3,020
Estimated expenses	$1,936
Gain (or loss)	$1,084

Month 7+

Estimated income	$5,048.40
Estimated expenses	$1,936
Gain (or loss)	$3,112.40

Because Janet's living expenses are $2,560, she obviously must have some cash on hand to carry her through the first six months. After examining her figures, she decided to remain at her job and save more money. Maybe in another year she will be ready to recalculate her forecasts and see if she will be in a better position to start her own business.

Step 6: Project Your Cash Flow

Because Janet decided not to start her service business, she did not get to step 6, the cash flow projection. Let's go through this step with David Donahue, another person who wants to be self-employed. First we'll go through the same five steps with his anticipated business enterprise and then take it through the sixth step. This will provide a slightly more complex picture of the process.

David is an excellent all-around automobile mechanic, is married and has two children, and wants to buy and operate his own auto repair shop. He is able to save money each month on two major budget items because his wife is a wise shopper and economical cook, and she also makes many of their children's clothing. Here is David's monthly personal budget.

Personal Monthly Budget

Food	$800
Clothing	$200
Mortgage payment	$1,300

House insurance	$60
House repairs	$100
Heating oil	$200
Property taxes	$240
Electricity and telephone	$280
Cell phone	$20
Internet	$40
Life insurance	$200
Health insurance	$380
Doctor, dentist, and drugs	$140
Children's allowances	$40
Income taxes	$280
Dry cleaning	$60
Haircuts, hairdresser	$120
Automobile insurance	$160
Automobile repairs	$40
Automobile payment	$340
Gasoline	$140
Recreation	$120
Gifts	$40
Emergencies	$80
Total	$5,380

This budget tells David that he has to repair enough cars to clear $5,380 every month. If he works six days a week, or twenty-five days each month on the average, he will have to make almost $240 a day after he pays all the expenses involved in running his auto repair shop.

In step 2, David drew up a statement of available capital or the amount of money he has to invest in the business.

Available Capital

Certificate of deposit	$20,000
Government bonds	$8,000
Silver coins	$1,600
Total	$29,600

David also has $3,120 in savings, which he did not include here because he wants to keep some cash on hand for emergencies. This is a wise move because in addition to needing capital to start your business, you may also require reserve cash to draw on during the first six or more months when you are developing your business. There may not be as much income as you expect or you might need more money for groceries or your other household expenses than the new business can initially earn.

Step 3, drawing up a list of capital expenditures, does not apply to David because he plans to buy an established auto repair business. He needs $20,000 for the down payment; the balance of $240,000 as a mortgage is to be paid in monthly installments over the next five years at $4,000 a month. The garage is stocked with all the heavy equipment and tools David will need and there are ample supplies of grease, small parts, and various accessories, so he doesn't have any other start-up expenses. Buying the business provides an added advantage: David knows how much the previous owner has been earning.

David's anticipated income is calculated in step 4. Since he is purchasing an established business, he knows what he can expect to take in each day, on the average. He plans to work by himself, at least at first, charging $60 an hour plus whatever parts might cost. Although he will make a little profit on parts, he decided not to include them in his earnings estimate because there is no way of knowing what he might sell. He feels safe in assuming that he will be busy all the time and that he can hire a mechanic to help him. He plans to work forty-four hours a week and have an assistant work only forty hours. Again this arithmetic is easy to do.

David

Income per day ($60/eight hours)	$480
Income per week ($60/forty-four hours)	$2,640
Income per month ($2,640/four weeks)	$10,560

David's Assistant

Income per day ($60/eight hours)	$480
Income per week ($480/five days)	$2,400
Income per month ($2,400/four weeks)	$9,600
Total monthly income (David and his assistant)	$20,160

Now that David knows his anticipated income, he can go to step 5, expenditures.

Monthly Operating Expenses

Supplies	$200
Electricity	$400
Heat	$200
($400 payments November, December, January, February, March, April)	
Telephone	$72
Insurance	$80
($960 payment due March)	
Mortgage payment	$4,000

Income taxes	$900
($10,800 payment due April)	
Bank repayment on truck	$600
Tow-truck license	$20
($240 payment due July)	
Property taxes	$1,200
($14,400 payment due May)	
Wages for mechanic	$5,520
Total	$13,192

This brings us to step 6, the final financial table you should construct, the cash flow projection, which is a combination business budget and cash flow. This is where you will project your expenses and income for the months to come so that you can plan ahead with as much knowledge as possible.

Cash Position Project Forecast

A word of caution about this final step: don't assume that your income and expense projections will always remain the same. Income may vary as business volume goes up or down. If David takes a two-week vacation, there will be $5,280 less to deposit in the bank those two weeks. When taxes, insurance, and other once-a-year payments come due, the checkbook will suddenly suffer. All these changes must be mapped out and anticipated. Unless you have saved up for the large annual expenses, you will be in serious trouble when they must be paid.

You will see in Table 5.1 that six months after he started his business, David's cash position varied during March, April, and May. The $36,492 figure for April is not devastating if each month he

Table 5.1 Cash Position Projection for March, April, and May

Expenses	March	April	May
Supplies	$200	$200	$200
Electricity	$400	$400	$400
Heat	$400	$400	$400
Telephone	$72	$72	$72
Insurance	$960	$80	$80
Mortgage payment	$4,000	$4,000	$4,000
Income taxes	$900	$10,800	$900
Bank repayment	$600	$600	$600
Tow-truck license	$20	$20	$20
Property taxes	$1,200	$14,400	$1,200
Wages for mechanic	$5,520	$5,520	$5,520
Total	$14,272	$36,492	$13,392

Income	March	April	May
Work charged at $15 per hour	$20,160	$20,160	$20,160
Gain (or loss)	$5,888	($16,332)	$6,768
Monthly personal budget	$5,380	$5,380	$5,380

has put aside $900 toward income taxes and $1,200 toward property taxes. It calls for willpower to do this, but it is the only way to run a business.

We know that David requires an income of $5,380 each month to meet his personal budget. His repair business easily covered his needs in March and May, but his family would have starved in April unless he had enough cash in the bank or could arrange a loan.

If you plan to open your own service business, take the time to go through the six financial planning steps suggested in this chapter. Be sure to construct a thorough and realistic forecast and see how you might make out for the first six or twelve months. A few hours spent doing this essential research and planning could mean the difference between success and failure.

6

RAISING MONEY

YOU KNOW FROM watching the news that consumer debt is at an all-time high. Much of this debt is caused by installment buying, as credit cards become easier to obtain and people continue to accumulate debt that often exceeds their ability to repay. Many people use several credit cards, obtaining funds from one to pay the balances on the others.

Hardly a day goes by without the mailbox holding new offers from credit card issuers with fantastic, hard-to-resist pitches such as "$100,000 credit limit," "Interest-free balance transfer," "Free checks for new cardholders," and so on. Unfortunately, these offers are too tempting for a lot of people, who use the cards to buy things they really don't need and couldn't otherwise afford.

You may have read about people using a credit card to help finance a business. Although this may seem to be a likely source of hard-to-obtain funds, it really is a bad idea to give into this temptation. It's much too easy to get in over your head with a credit card and then be obligated to repay the balance at a very high interest rate. If you can't obtain the capital you need from the sources discussed in this chapter, you probably should think about delaying starting your own service business.

If you own a home and are not saddled with a large mortgage, you might be able to add to your present mortgage or obtain an equity loan. However, most financial planners would probably not recommend this. A home is so essential to a family's well-being that it's usually not advisable to put the property at risk with the obligation to repay debt.

So, without credit cards and mortgages as borrowing possibilities, where can you turn for the money you'll need to start your business? In this chapter we'll consider these options: banks, the U.S. Small Business Administration, the Canada Small Business Financing program, and friends and family.

Banks

Banks may prove the best source of capital for your new business, but you should bear in mind that they are subject to both state or provincial and federal banking regulations. They must be careful to operate within those rules, limitations that tend to make them conservative.

Applications approved by the loan officer are usually reviewed by a committee. Although making a good impression on the loan officer may influence the final decision, many factors enter into the granting or refusing of a loan, so don't be discouraged if you are turned down. Your service may be one to which the bank does not normally extend credit. You may have better luck at another bank.

Remember that banks are competitive. Especially when interest rates are high, it pays to shop around to try to obtain your loan at the lowest possible rate. However, if most local banks are not enthusiastic about extending you a loan, you may have to accept a higher rate at the one that will help you.

Banks expect you, the borrower, to put up capital, too. This is because they believe if you also have a financial stake in the business, you will work harder to make it succeed. This investment on your part is often called *venture capital.*

The loan application that the bank will require you to complete is sometimes referred to as the *loan package.* It must be truthful, give all details of the proposed business, and be convincing. Perhaps the primary reason that loans are turned down is because the loan packages are poorly or inadequately prepared. When you are given the application to fill out, be sure you understand exactly what is expected of you. Ask if any additional information not called for on the application would be helpful. Spend time on your application, and avoid the temptation to overstate or stray from the truth.

Types of Loans

Most banks extend three types of loans: short-term, intermediate-term, and long-term loans.

Short-term loans are written for thirty, sixty, or ninety days but no longer than one year. They can usually be renewed, but some banks ask to have them repaid for approximately a month before being renewed so that the state bank examiners will see that technically they have been repaid. Small businesses can generally obtain short-term loans fairly easily, especially if they have good collateral.

Intermediate-term loans are generally for three to five years and are more difficult to obtain. It is necessary to prepare a full proposal giving a complete picture of your business when you apply for these loans.

Long-term loans are for five or ten years and are not available for small businesses.

Although applying for a bank loan may seem like an enormous step, don't be nervous or intimidated. Remember that the bank is in business to make money, and lending funds is one of its principal ways of earning a profit. Go to the bank with all the information you can gather about your proposed service, your financial requirements, your anticipated income and expenses, and how you plan to spend the money. Be sure you are prepared to explain how you expect to repay the loan. Be ready to answer all kinds of questions honestly and accurately. If you cannot answer a question, admit it, but offer to obtain the requested information. If you establish a good rapport with the loan officer, he or she will probably be willing to help you with the process.

U.S. Small Business Administration

The U.S. Small Business Administration (SBA) is not the only government agency that extends loans to entrepreneurs, but it is the one you should consult first. The SBA grants loans to borrowers by guaranteeing loans made by your bank and sometimes by making loans directly to borrowers. There is no minimum amount for which you may apply, and the maximum amount the SBA will guarantee varies from $150,000 to $500,000, depending on the type of loan.

How to Apply for a Loan

Your loan application must include a written loan proposal. Make your best presentation in the initial loan proposal and application, because you may not get a second opportunity.

Begin your proposal with a cover letter or executive summary. Clearly and briefly explain who you are, your business background, the nature of your business, the amount and purpose of your loan request, your requested terms of repayment, how the funds will benefit your business, and how you will repay the loan. Keep this cover page simple and direct.

There are many different loan proposal formats, so you may want to contact your commercial lender to determine which is best for you. When writing your proposal, don't assume the reader is familiar with your industry or your individual business. Include industry-specific details so your reader can understand how your particular business is run and what industry trends affect it.

Basic Requirements

Although SBA-qualifying standards are more flexible than those of other types of loans, lenders will generally ask for certain information before deciding to use an SBA loan program. Generally, the following documentation will be needed to evaluate your request:

- **Business profile.** This is a document describing the type of business, annual sales, number of employees, length of time in business, and ownership.
- **Loan request.** This is a description of how loan funds will be used and should include the purpose, amount, and type of loan.
- **Collateral.** This is a description of collateral offered to secure the loan, including equity in the business, borrowed funds, and available cash.
- **Business financial statements.** These are complete financial statements for the past three years and current interim financial statements.

• **Personal financial statements.** These are the financial statements of owners, partners, officers, and stockholders owning 20 percent or more of the business.

Take all this material to your banker and ask for a direct bank loan. If denied, ask if the bank would make the loan under SBA's Loan Guarantee Plan or Immediate Participation Plan. If the bank is interested in an SBA-guaranteed or participation loan, ask the banker to contact SBA about your application. In most cases of guaranteed or participation loans, SBA deals directly with the bank.

If neither of these loans is available, contact the SBA directly. There are more than one hundred district and regional SBA field offices; you can locate the one nearest you by visiting www.sba.gov.

Canada Small Business Financing Program

The Canada Small Business Financing (CSBF) program is part of Industry Canada. Under the program, you can apply for a loan at any bank, credit union, *caisse populaire*, or other financial institution. There are approximately 1,540 participating lenders with about 15,200 points of service in all provinces and territories. Lenders are responsible for all credit decisions, making the loans, and providing loan funds.

Eligible Small Businesses

To be eligible for a loan under the program, a business must meet the following criteria:

• The business must be carried on in Canada.
• The business must be for gain or profit.

• For an existing business, the estimated gross annual revenues must not exceed $5 million for the fiscal year during which the CSBF loan is approved.

• For a new business, at the time the CSBF loan is approved, the estimated annual gross revenues must not be expected to exceed $5 million during the first fifty-two weeks of operation.

Financial institutions can finance up to 90 percent of the cost of asset acquisition or asset improvement. The maximum loan amount a small business can access under this program is $250,000.

Visit http://strategis.ic.gc.ca/csbfa for complete information about the CSBF program and to download the required application forms.

Friends and Family

The Shakespearian adage, "Neither a borrower nor a lender be" is usually good advice when it comes to transactions with friends, but there are circumstances when a personal loan makes sense. Many people are glad to help a friend make a start as an entrepreneur. Some enjoy the idea of investing extra savings in a new business, and some see it as a short-term method of earning a good return on their money.

It's important to remember that even though the lender might be a close friend or relative, you will still have to pay interest, at least as much as the current bank interest rate. You can't expect someone to withdraw funds from a high-interest certificate of deposit, money market fund, mutual fund, or other investment and not expect to earn as much, if not more, because of the added risk involved.

If you have been turned down by banks and the SBA or CSBF program, you may be able to find an individual acceptable to the bank who will agree to cosign your loan application. Bear in mind, though, that in the event you default on the loan, the cosigner is liable for the amount due.

Most likely you will only need to complete the bank's loan application and talk with the loan officer. If you are requesting a large sum of money, you'll need to prepare a fairly detailed proposal giving full data about the business, including its financial condition, operating statistics, forecasts, and so forth.

If you are unsuccessful in interesting either the banks or the SBA or CSBF program in lending you money for your service business, it's possible that either you did not present yourself properly or your idea is not sound. If you are still determined to move forward with your business plan, you might consider involving members of your family. Even if you prefer not to borrow money from relatives, putting any such transaction on a strictly business basis, on the same terms that a bank would require, and living up to your agreement to pay interest on time and make repayments as promised should keep peace in the family and help you realize your goals.

7

Getting the Word Out

YOU'VE DONE THE research, secured financing, set up the company, and ordered your business cards. Now, how do you let people know that you're in business? There are several ways of telling people you are ready, eager, and qualified to serve them. But because businesses are so varied, not every method may be right for you.

Before you do anything to promote your service, learn something about advertising and promotion so you don't strike out blind in your campaign. See the Suggested Reading at the back of this book for resources, and if possible, ask for advice from business acquaintances who might be able to help you with this important activity.

Advertising

There are different types of advertising for you to consider. Evaluate each carefully to see which types fit best based on your budget and the amount of time you can devote to advertising.

Print Advertising

Print advertising is a good way to reach the public, particularly for a service business. If you choose to advertise in the newspaper, you have two options: a display ad, which is a regular ad placed next to the news items; or a classified ad, a small two-, three-, or four-line advertisement that appears in the classified section. Which will be more effective depends on the newspaper's readership and whether the subscribers regularly look through the classifieds and would be likely to see your ad. If this is not the case where you live, a display ad might be more effective, provided you run it several times.

If you decide to place a newspaper ad, choose your local paper and, if you can afford it, the local papers of one or two neighboring areas. To save money, you can advertise in *The PennySaver*, which you may already be familiar with. It's delivered weekly to homes and businesses in most areas of the United States and Canada. People consult it to find service businesses, and each publication is distributed to a number of communities, saving you the expense of placing individual ads in different towns.

You can also place an ad in the yellow pages. You can choose a display ad or just the one- or two-line alphabetical entry in your business category, which should be free with your phone number.

Many churches publish weekly or monthly bulletins that include small ads for local businesses. This can be an excellent way to get started, especially if you are already familiar to members of the congregation. Many churches and local stores will also allow you to display a flyer or business card on a community bulletin board.

Direct Mail

Direct mail is another option, but it can be a time-consuming and expensive way to reach people. In addition to printing your advertising material, you must compile a list of prospects, address envelopes, stuff and seal them, and, finally, pay for postage, all of which can take considerable time and money. The success of an advertising campaign depends on the effectiveness of your advertising piece as well as on the list of names selected to receive it. Unless the recipients are people who are likely to want and use your service, your advertising dollars are wasted—a baby-clothing boutique won't find many customers in a community made up mostly of senior citizens or single, working people.

The Internet

The Internet can be one of the most effective advertising tools you will use. You can have your company listed in various Internet directories geared toward specific businesses, and telephone directories are available online as well.

However, perhaps the best advertising you can do on the Internet is to establish your own website. An effective website should include information about the company, such as the specific services you offer, the locations you serve, the equipment you use, and any rave reviews from customers. Be sure to include some graphics and perhaps a photo of you or of your office if clients will visit you there.

You can also register your site with a search engine or two. This is generally a free service, and doing so will put your website at the top of the list when a customer searches in your business category.

If you don't have the skills or know anyone who can design a site for you, there are services available that will set up your site for a reasonable fee. Your telephone company might also offer a Web-design service for small business customers. If you'd like to try your hand at Web design but need some guidance, see the Suggested Reading section for books that might be helpful.

Personal Contact and Word of Mouth

Delivering your message personally can be particularly effective. Tell everyone you know about your new business, and ask them to spread the word. Carry business cards with you at all times, and give a few to close friends and family members you trust to mention your business to appropriate prospective customers.

Since you never know when an opportunity might arise to promote your business, you should always be professional yet friendly when you meet people. If you do give a business card to someone who asks for one or who seems particularly interested in your company, make a note of his or her name so that you'll recognize it when he or she calls for an appointment or comes in for service.

Referrals

This is the best advertising! Because someone who has used and liked your service recommended you, you've got a new customer at no cost to you. But the only way to get referrals is to consistently give the kind of service that satisfies customers or even exceeds their expectations. When customers pay their bill, thank them, hand them a business card, and ask them to tell their friends and relatives about your service. If a client offers to give you the names and addresses of friends to contact, don't waste any time—call them!

It takes time before referrals start coming in, but when they do, you can be quite sure you have a customer ready to do business.

Public Relations

The purpose of public relations is to establish the best possible image of your company in the public eye. Don't worry, you won't need to hire a PR firm to promote your business. If you familiarize yourself with the three basic components of public relations—publicity, promotion, and good deeds—you'll be able to get the word out yourself.

Publicity

Publicity is news that spreads the word about your business in an attempt to build goodwill. It is different from advertising because it involves more than just buying ad space. A publicity announcement would involve some news item in which your business is involved; the story printed in the papers that names your company is publicity.

You probably won't be doing much publicity work at first, unless your company becomes involved in the other aspects of PR, which are described here.

Promotion

Promotion is any special activity aimed at gaining attention. It does not have to benefit the public but is simply a way of calling attention to your service so the person seeing it will pay attention to any publicity or advertising message that follows.

Macy's annual Thanksgiving Day parade is an example of promotion. The parade isn't an advertisement for the store's merchandise. It isn't publicity, since it doesn't give any information. But it is a promotion, because it's part of an overall public relations program that aims to create goodwill for the store.

Other examples of promotion include giving away balloons with your name on them, having a float in a local parade, or sponsoring a local Little League baseball team.

In other words, it is anything that draws attention and allows people to see your business name.

Good Deeds

Spending money to advertise is promotion, getting news coverage is publicity, making a contribution to the Boy Scouts or Girl Scouts is public relations by good deed. There is no direct return from such public relations, but this is building goodwill.

Public relations carries over to the operation of your business, too, where it is more accurately called *customer relations*. Good customer relations may be a good deed such as: giving a "baker's dozen" rolls, wiping off a customer's car after you have serviced it, or sending a brief thank-you note to a customer after you have completed an expensive job.

If you think carefully, you can probably come up with even more ideas for acts of goodwill. Can you volunteer your carpentry company's service to a local church group that renovates homes for low-income families? How about donating your service as a personal chef to the residents of the local senior citizens' residence community? Does your town have an organization that accepts used clothing to be recycled for women who are returning to the workforce? If so, you might consider donating your dressmaking and alteration services to help these women look and feel their best in their new business endeavors.

In summary, good public relations includes many factors, such as maintaining a business presence that is a credit to the neighborhood, providing a neighborhood bulletin board outside your store or office, volunteering time to a community activity, and doing anything else that will enhance your image as both a good citizen and a good businessperson.

8

A DIFFERENT LIFESTYLE

MAKING THE CHANGE from high school, college, or a secure job into a new business may well prove to be one of the most significant and bewildering steps you will take in your life. While it is certainly challenging, fun, and exciting, it can also be your ticket to possible financial and personal problems, cash flow forecasts, meetings, and a seemingly endless work schedule.

At first these new demands on your time, patience, and energy might seem overwhelming, and you may even doubt your ability to handle them. You should realize that starting a business will almost always lead to changes in other areas of your life as well. Since some changes are inevitable, why not allow your new business to act as a catalyst for a personal review that might lead to some positive changes in these other areas as well? Even though the patterns of your life will change, there's no reason that these changes can't be pleasurable as well as profitable.

Need for Self-Discipline

Some people exercise self-discipline in everything they do, but they're generally in the minority. Most of us just aren't that focused on maintaining strict self-discipline in every aspect of our lives. However, as a business owner, you're about to take a great risk by assuming command of a new company, and you will need all the mental direction you can muster. Here are the principal areas where exercising self-discipline can prove exceedingly helpful in your new venture.

Remembering Names

Nothing flatters people more than being greeted by someone who remembers their name. The ability to remember names adds greatly to the favorable impression you make on people. If you operate a service business where customers come to you, such as a delicatessen or video rental store, your regular customers will appreciate being recognized and called by name when they visit your establishment. Many people continue to patronize a business primarily because they feel comfortable and welcome there.

Preparing a Daily Agenda

Most well-organized businesspeople end their workday by making an agenda of items to be attended to the following day. It serves as a good guideline for a day's activity, making certain that no immediate responsibility is overlooked, and it also provides a blueprint for action. In addition, it's a useful check at the end of the day to make sure you haven't forgotten any tasks. Working with an agenda takes discipline, but once you form the habit, you'll be surprised at how it can contribute to your efficiency.

Keeping Up Your Personal and Office Appearance

It's a good rule to see that you are presentable at all times and make the best possible impression on your customers as well as your employees. Along the same lines, your office should be impeccable, which means being sure that your desk is neat, the floor is clean, and the wastebaskets aren't overflowing. It's easy to put off straightening up until tomorrow, but today might be the day an important customer unexpectedly visits.

Even if customers don't come to your office, keeping a neat, organized working environment will help you feel more productive. If you travel to your customers' locations, be sure that you always look presentable. Even if you work in a hands-on area such as home repair or plumbing, you should try to make a clean impression at each appointment. Keep an extra shirt or uniform in your truck for emergency changes—and make sure your shoes or boots are clean so you don't leave dirt in the customer's home.

Taking Care of Yourself

Another way that self-discipline can help you as a business owner is by making sure to take care of yourself, physically and mentally. One of the best things you can do is to follow a healthy diet. You might think this sounds silly, especially if you are young and healthy and have just spent four years on a typical undergraduate diet of pizza and burgers. Fast food and coffee might have been fine for your college days, but once you're a business owner, you'll realize how much better maintaining a healthy diet can make you feel.

Planning and starting your service business will put a lot of demands on you, and you'll need to be clearheaded and wide awake to be successful. Eat a healthy breakfast (not doughnuts!). Try to take the time for a proper lunch away from work. Even eating a sandwich or salad outdoors will give you a welcome break from sitting in the office or driving between appointments. Keep fruit and protein bars handy for snacks, and have lots of bottled water around, as well.

It's also a good idea to schedule time for exercise into your day. If you're already a fitness fan, you won't want to give up your time at the gym or on the track. If you aren't, try to take a walk each day to clear your mind and keep you fit. Exercise is also a great way to relax your muscles after several hours at the computer or behind the wheel.

If you find yourself becoming mentally stressed, think about the ways you can relax your mind, even if it is only for a few minutes. Step away from your work long enough to flip through a magazine, surf the Web, do a crossword puzzle—whatever it is that takes your mind off business and helps you relax.

Need for Managerial Aptitude and Experience

The purpose of this chapter is certainly not to discourage you—just the opposite. It is intended to help you understand the importance of not starting your own business until you have done the personal self-searching and preliminary marketing and financial planning that every intelligent prospective businessperson should do.

Let's be realistic. A study of a million business failures over a period of a century revealed that 90 percent of them were due to lack of managerial aptitude and experience. Furthermore, half of all new businesses fail within their first year, and five years later 80 percent of the rest have disappeared.

"This won't happen to me," you think, and we certainly hope that you're right. And it shouldn't happen if you have the aptitude and experience necessary to manage your own business and will seriously consider the suggestions offered in this book. Above all, don't rush into a decision. Your goal is to establish a business that will be profitable, bring you personal satisfaction, and last as long as you want to operate it. This goal is not attainable overnight.

Get-Rich Schemes to Avoid

"Lazy Millionaire Wants to Share the Wealth," "Up to $30,000 in Six Weeks Guaranteed or Your Money Back: $12 for Starter Kit," "You, Too, Can Become Rich in a Short Time," "Work from Home and Earn $5,000 a Month."

You see ads like these all the time in newspapers and magazines. Television commercials abound with work-at-home offers, and infomercials keep us up at night telling us how to make millions in real estate. Some advertisers are so wealthy, they say, that they want to share their secrets with you and offer you a thirty-day "risk-free" trial of their product or service. That's fine, as long as you remember to return the cumbersome package containing the ten DVDs that didn't change your life after all—if you forget, the full price of the item will be charged to your credit card.

As for the starter kits and other products that offer surefire money-making tips, you'll find that most of them are useless. In general, beware of offers that do any or all of the following:

- State that prior experience, special skills, or knowledge is unnecessary

- Promise you will earn incredible sums of money
- Require that you buy instructions or merchandise before they tell you what the plan is or how it works
- Assure you that there is a guaranteed market for your services

One exception is some of the advertisements offering to franchise a service or a product. Although some are certainly suspect, many are credible offerings. Because of the popularity and prevalence of franchise opportunities, be sure to read Chapter 14, which tells you more about this interesting field.

Time Trap

One of the hidden dangers of many service businesses is the *time trap*. This refers to the twenty-four-hour day within which you must sleep, dress, eat, do household and personal chores, and have some recreation. If you are a true workaholic, you will perhaps have twelve hours a day for business, and if you stick to the job six days a week, you'll have some seventy-two hours to manage and operate your business.

That sounds like plenty of time to put into a business, doesn't it? It is—more than enough. You should allow time to spend with your family, see friends, or just read a book. The point is that in some service businesses, even seventy-two hours a week may not be sufficient to enable you to earn an adequate income for your needs. Your earnings may be limited by the number of hours you can work.

Take a hairstylist, carpenter, or plumber, for example, who may work nine hours a day and charge $25 an hour. Even though they work all nine hours during the day, none of these service people can earn more than $225 unless they work during the evening as well. The time trap is especially cruel to craftspeople because many of their handcrafted products require so many hours to produce that their price tags are higher than the public will pay.

Unlike the craftsperson, a hairstylist, carpenter, or plumber can hire an assistant at a lower hourly wage than he or she charges customers, and the difference spells added income. Owners of other businesses may find ways to augment their income, too. But regardless of what you do, you cannot stop the clock or cram more jobs into an hour than you can physically handle.

One final thought about the time trap. If you can't plan for the most constructive use of your time and discipline yourself to use every moment to your advantage, you should probably find a job where someone else will arrange your working schedule and tell you what to do.

The first eight chapters of this book covered the nuts and bolts of the service industry; now it's time to follow them with examples of how people have actually started a wide variety of service businesses. It's impossible to cover every type of service, but the examples in the following chapters should familiarize you with the principles of starting and operating any company.

You will find success stories about world-famous companies and local businesses that offer a range of services. These real-life examples should provide further inspiration as you plan and research your own service business career.

9

FEEDING THE PUBLIC

MOST OF US enjoy going out to eat, and sometimes eating out is a necessity if we're running errands and can't get home for lunch or are traveling. Even the smallest rural towns generally have some sort of eatery, perhaps a counter in the general store where customers can order coffee and a slice of pie. Dining establishments make up one of the largest service industries, one that is expected to grow as the population increases. But before you start planning the menu or shopping for a chef's toque, read on to learn about the ins and outs of running a restaurant business.

Of all the smaller service businesses, probably none has a higher percentage of failure than eating establishments, which range from tiny holes-in-the-wall that serve burgers, chili, coffee, and cake to the finer, more expensive restaurants in many cities. Most restaurant failures are due to owners not conducting the necessary market research and lacking enough initial capital to keep the door open long enough to get established. Inexperience is another cause, especially among entrepreneurs of more expensive restaurants. Too many owners make the mistake of thinking that an experienced chef and manager will provide the expertise they lack and therefore guarantee success. However, if a proper market survey and provision of sufficient capital have not been undertaken, no amount of professional know-how will save the day—or your business.

None of this is intended to discourage you but rather to encourage you to be fully prepared before you enter this type of business. If your ultimate goal is to open a high-end restaurant or to work in one as a chef or manager, you should seriously consider getting some formal training. Courses in food preparation and restaurant management are available at some private or state universities and community colleges, as well as through adult education courses.

Another training option is to attend a culinary school. There are a number of culinary institutes throughout North America, such as the Culinary Institute of America in Hyde Park, New York; Johnson and Wales University in Providence, Rhode Island; Loyalist College in Belleville, Ontario; and George Brown College in Toronto.

Most restaurant owners have worked in various food-related jobs before taking the plunge and opening their own businesses. Many start as busboys or waiters; some are bartenders or managers. If possible, you should try to gain experience in as many areas of the business as possible. This will also help you better understand your employees' needs.

As our society becomes increasingly affluent and food conscious, as well as more inclined to eat away from home than ever before, opportunities for developing your own restaurant have never been better. Factor into the equation our growing interest in different types of foods and different dining atmospheres: gourmet, ethnic, and regional foods; specialty foods such as pizza or bagels; a breakfast and/or lunch diner. People who entertain privately often hire catering services, and lots of busy people use take-out services.

With all of these options, if you're serious about a food service business, you should be able to find something that suits you.

Restaurants

Let's take a look at two completely different types of restaurants to see how they began and how they've grown since their owners' initial endeavors.

Chez Panisse

Some of the best restaurants on the West Coast are those known as cafes, which began by catering largely to gourmet diners who had traveled in Europe and sought the same type of dining here.

One of the most popular of these restaurants is San Francisco's Chez Panisse Cafe and Restaurant. Opened in 1971, it soon became a dinner restaurant specializing in French dishes with a menu that changed nightly based on the season and the highest-quality local ingredients available. Under the guidance of Alice Waters, its chef and cofounder, it gradually achieved a national reputation for excellence and originality. Prices are moderate and the atmosphere is charming and unusual. Some evenings five hundred or more customers converge on the small, two-story building on Berkeley's Shattuck Avenue, attesting to the restaurant's popularity nearly forty years after its opening.

In recalling the restaurant's gradual growth over the years, Alice Waters reflected, "We started as a group of friends interested in food and cooking and learned as we went along. We started with very little money and just persisted until we were able to begin reinvesting our earnings back into the restaurant and the building. I think we did well because we knew what we were trying to achieve, and we were willing to go for it. I don't know if this is a blueprint for success, but it worked for us."

In addition to her work as a restaurateur, in 1996 Alice Waters celebrated the twenty-fifth anniversary of her restaurant by starting the Chez Panisse Foundation. The mission of the foundation is to establish a nationwide public school curriculum that includes hands-on experience in school kitchens, gardens, and lunchrooms. The goal is to inspire students to choose healthy food and to understand its impact on them and their environment.

Alice Waters is also the author or coauthor of more than a dozen cookbooks, many based on recipes from Chez Panisse.

The Golden Arches

You certainly don't need an introduction to McDonald's, the world's largest fast-food chain and franchise operation. It is included here because it shows what imagination and hard work can achieve within a short time; and who knows, you may get an idea for a different service business!

You are so accustomed to McDonald's that you've probably not thought about how the phenomenon began; you might be surprised to learn that there was a time when a McDonald's didn't exist on nearly every street.

Back in 1954, Maurice and Richard McDonald were running a hamburger stand in San Bernardino, California, where they used the Multimixer, a device that could whirl five milk shakes at the same time. In fact, the brothers used eight Multimixers, which meant that they could make forty shakes simultaneously. When

Ray Kroc, the exclusive distributor of the Multimixer, heard about the number of machines the McDonald brothers were using, he traveled to California to see the operation for himself. He was so excited by what he saw that he asked the brothers if he could open a similar stand somewhere outside of California.

The McDonalds weren't especially anxious to expand beyond the six outlets they had already licensed in California, but they finally agreed. In 1955, Des Plaines, Illinois, in the Chicago area, saw the first McDonald's outside the Golden State. Kroc's optimism paid off quickly, and six years later, when there were 250 McDonald's across the United States, he bought the business from the brothers for $2.7 billion and proceeded to expand McDonald's into the business it is today, with restaurants in more than one hundred countries.

If you are interested in the restaurant business, be sure to read about the Beau Jo's Restaurants in Chapter 14. This is a good example of how a business owner turned his single restaurant into a thriving franchise.

Catering

A catering service is first cousin to the restaurant business. By comparison it requires little capital and does not call for a large payroll because you hire employees only when you need them. Following is an example of a successful catering service business.

Ladyfingers

Andrea Bell says that she has enjoyed cooking since she was a child, and this early interest finally led her to open her own catering business—Ladyfingers.

Once her children were in school, Andrea had more time for some of her hobbies, which included the harpsichord, reading, and cooking. First she taught a nutrition course in the adult education program in Kennebunk, Maine, where she was living. Next she taught a cooking class, and finally she started her own business.

Kennebunk and neighboring Kennebunkport are affluent communities that were ready for a good catering service. Andrea's first client was the mother of a friend, and business gradually grew as guests who attended parties that Andrea catered hired Ladyfingers for their own events. She arranged to be interviewed by the local newspaper, and that publicity helped spread the word. Before long the phone started ringing and she was busy. Andrea soon added businesses to her clientele, catering a large and elaborate cocktail party hosted by a bank.

Andrea's original investment was small because she worked out of her kitchen and purchased only some extra utensils, baking sheets, and other cooking aids. Her first jobs were done in homes where all the necessary china, glassware, and silver were furnished by the client. Later, at larger parties such as the bank affair, it was necessary to rent dishes, glasses, silver, tables, chairs, and so forth. As the parties grew in size, Andrea hired assistants. She trained them carefully and even sewed serving uniforms for them to wear.

Andrea follows a specific process when she is contacted about a new job. First she makes an appointment to visit the client at home (if that is where the party will be held) to discuss all the details of the event. She makes floor plans of the rooms that she later uses to brief her staff on where each will be stationed and what their duties will be. She then draws up a contract that details the menu, the number of people to be served, any other pertinent details, and the price. Based on her experience, Andrea says, "I found that this was a must because some people remember things that were not agreed upon—and it could be difficult."

Learning how to price jobs came with experience and having some basic accounting knowledge. Andrea calculates the cost of food, adds a percentage to cover preparation, and bases labor costs on the estimated number of hours to be spent on the job. The rate is computed to return the hourly rate that she wants to clear for herself.

Ladyfingers's service includes such extras as arranging flowers, purchasing ice for drinks, hiring a bartender, and renting tables, chairs, and other accessories as needed. Upon request, Ladyfingers's personnel will take guests' wraps as they arrive. Passing drinks and hors d'oeuvres among the guests and waiting on tables requires assistants who are poised and pleasant.

Andrea is able to purchase some items wholesale but recommends buying perishables at a good market. Volume is a factor, since wholesalers are not interested in an order unless you buy in bulk. Additionally, if you operate out of your home, there may be zoning restrictions that prevent trucks from delivering to a residence, as well as neighbors who might object to the disruption.

She stresses the importance of checking to see whether your city, state, or province requires a license or permit to run such a business. And be sure to have enough insurance. As Andrea says, "You never know when someone working for Ladyfingers might break a valuable dish or piece of art by accident."

Andrea has a closet filled with equipment and an extra second-hand refrigerator and freezer to be used when she has a large number of hors d'oeuvres and other foods to prepare in advance.

"You know, the best part about this business is that you just pick it up from one place and move it to another," she observed. "When

we moved to Providence, I put Ladyfingers in several cartons—
except for the refrigerator and freezer—and it was no problem
whatever to get going again after we were settled."

Lunch Baskets

Karen Sullivan loves to cook. Her friends look forward to her dinner parties, and she is often asked to bring one of her specialties
when she visits someone's home. After a career in the music industry, she worked for several years at an exclusive club in an upscale
Florida community. When she left that job, she kept looking for
something else that would interest her and always came back to
cooking.

Karen thought about the different ways she could make cooking her new career and considered such options as personal chef or
caterer. These ideas didn't seem quite right, and then she found
something that suits both her interests and her lifestyle. She pre-
pares fresh lunches that she sells each day in the downtown business district.

Based on her cooking experience, Karen already had most of the
recipes she needed to run a successful lunch business. She offers a
variety of healthy salads, sandwiches made with the freshest available ingredients, and satisfying soups.

Karen got started by self-printing an attractive flyer that she distributed to businesses in the area announcing her new enterprise,
and word-of-mouth advertising has been one of her biggest boosts.
She didn't need any substantial start-up money because she works
from home. Her biggest purchase was a second refrigerator, where
she can store her Lunch Basket provisions separate from her family's food, and a refrigerated vending table that she purchased from
a restaurant supply store.

Karen has the required license that allows her to sell food on the street, where she sets her vending table each weekday. She also accepts advance orders—sometimes a group of employees are planning a special luncheon celebration and want something different from the ordinary cafeteria fare. Karen packages her selections in small attractive baskets.

The business fits well into Karen's lifestyle. She plans menus and does preparation work in the evenings, and each morning she assembles the meals that she'll sell that day. She generally sells from 11:00 A.M. to 2:00 P.M. "I love this business," she says. "I get to practice my favorite pastime, and to see people coming back and telling me how much they've enjoyed something I cooked is so gratifying. And I get to spend part of my day outdoors. This is perfect!"

Family Enterprise

Even though the success story of Fred and Louis Ruiz of Tulare, California, can be strictly termed that of a service business only during one brief part of its history, it is nevertheless an inspirational one that should encourage you as you strive to make your own new enterprise succeed.

Louis Ruiz is a Mexican native who came to Los Angeles as a child. Before serving in World War II, he owned a grocery store, and after his discharge from the army, he joined the Flintkote Corporation with the expectation of making a lifetime career there.

What Louis really wanted more than anything else was to be his own boss. He soon resigned from Flintkote to open a clothing store, and he also sold sweaters door to door. As he traveled he saw that Mexican food was becoming popular in the United States, so he began cooking wheat-flour tortillas at home to sell, an endeavor that didn't work out so well. This began a long entrepreneurial journey during which he gave up the unsuccessful tortilla business, went to work in a grocery store, and again struck out on his own, this time with a service business delivering groceries.

His son Fred joined him, and soon they were back in the food business making frozen enchiladas that they produced at home using their own equipment. When their small operation didn't pass state meat processing standards, they turned to nonmeat enchiladas. But grocers complained that there was not enough filling, the frost on the plastic wrapping discouraged sales, there were packaging and marketing questions to resolve, and there was the ever-present need for more capital.

They persisted, however, and solved their problems. As the business grew, they arranged to rent a commercial freezing plant. But first they had to raise $14,000, which they did by selling stock to Tulare residents, and then used the money to rehabilitate the leased space. Before long they had five employees and an efficient operation, but they still found themselves facing a serious cash flow problem.

Unwilling to give up, Louis proposed making and selling tamales. In a short time, they had installed small heating ovens in five grocery stores to warm their wares. The idea caught on and sales shot up, passing the half million dollar mark.

During this time, however, the state of California had asked the U.S. Department of Agriculture to take over food inspection duties, and the Ruiz's plant didn't meet the stricter federal standards. Their choice was simple—close the business or rebuild.

Fred and Louis Ruiz never considered the first choice and chose to rebuild their business. Fred applied to the Small Business Administration and a local bank and secured loans totaling $635,000—

the cost of a new plant. Eventually the company had more than two hundred employees and annual sales of approximately $20 million, making Ruiz Food Products the second-largest producer of frozen foods in the West.

In 1999, Ruiz Foods was named Minority Manufacturing Firm of the Year by the San Francisco office of the Minority Business Development Agency, U.S. Department of Commerce. Four years later, the company was named 2003 Large Business of the Year by the Dinuba (CA) Chamber of Commerce and was visited by President George W. Bush.

The company's products have been featured on television's Food Network. In 2006 Fred's son, F. Bryce Ruiz, was named president and CEO of Ruiz Foods. In addition, the city of Dinuba dedicated Louis F. Ruiz Park, and Fred Ruiz was inducted in the Frozen Food Hall of Fame.

A Final Word

If you like the idea of offering a food-related service, some of the businesses profiled in this chapter might spark an idea for your own company. Whether you'd like to cook or to manage a restaurant, there are many options for profitable service businesses in the food industry. Think about your personality, whether you'd like to serve people directly or be behind the scenes, and how you'd like to present your service. If you have the ability and determination, you can create a successful career in this sought-after service industry.

10

Travel: A
Fast-Growing Industry

People everywhere are on the go. Whether for pleasure or business, more of us are interested in travel than ever before. After a decline following the terrorist attacks of September 11, 2001, travelers are back at the airports, railroad terminals, and ship ports. And many of us are taking road trips in the family car.

All of these trips are possible because the hospitality industry provides homes away from home. Many hotels and motels are conveniently located near major highways or airports, and accommodations thrive in resort areas that line lakes and coastal towns as well as mountain areas.

There's no question that service is the hallmark of the travel empire. Take any aspect of a trip, and you find that employees are doing their best to give customers the finest service possible. The taxi driver who takes you to the airport or train station, the porter hustling your bags to the check-in counter, the flight attendant or conductor who helps you to your seat, the men and women on the flight deck committed to getting you to your destination safely and on time—all of these professionals are dedicated to providing the best possible service to customers.

Hotels are equally service oriented, and all employees are carefully trained in attending to every need of every guest. High turnover in many establishments makes this difficult to maintain but easier for those seeking a hospitality career to find an opening. Glance through any travel magazine and you will see the lengths to which management will go to attract and please its clientele.

Ins and Outs of Innkeeping

Many people are attracted to the service business of running an inn, especially one in an idyllic location such as the mountains or seashore. It's easy to romanticize themselves in the role of innkeeper who greets guests warmly, shows them to their rooms, ushers them to their tables for dinner, chats with them about local attractions, and serves a homey breakfast the next morning. And they'd get paid for doing it!

In reality, you can't overlook the cleaning and bed making, menu planning, food buying, and meal preparing and serving. And don't forget maintenance; daily bookkeeping; ongoing hiring, training, and supervising of staff; advertising; worrying about cash flow; and wondering when you are going to get a good night's sleep.

Today there are four principal types of accommodations: hotels, motels, bed-and-breakfasts, and smaller inns. All have the same purpose, which is to provide travelers with comfortable accommodations and good food. But given the number of duties involved in running one of these establishments, you might be wondering how you would ever make a start, let alone become a success.

Take heart. The great Hilton chain of hotels is a tribute to its founder, Conrad Hilton, who started in Cisco, Texas, by buying the old Mobley Hotel in 1919 for $5,000. He expanded gradually but nearly lost everything during the Depression. He survived and gradually began to prosper, acquiring hotels like the Sir Francis Drake in San Francisco and others in the West. His greatest ambition was to own New York City's Waldorf-Astoria, with its famed Peacock Alley and its twin towers overlooking Park Avenue. He carried a picture of the Waldorf in his wallet for years and finally, in 1950, realized his dream. Today Hilton Hotels are among the finest in the world.

Perhaps you prefer the humbler start of the Marriott chain, which traces its beginnings to Washington, DC, when John Willard Marriott and his new bride opened a franchised A&W Root Beer stand in 1927. Scorching temperatures made for good business that first summer, and once winter arrived and customers disappeared, Marriott lost no time switching from cold to hot fare and nailed a sign over the stand that read, "Hot Shoppe." The Marriotts served hot tamales and hearty chili based on recipes they obtained from a cook at the Mexican embassy. Residents liked the new Mexican food, and before long the Marriotts opened a number of Hot Shoppes around the city.

Ten years later they went into the airline catering business with a contract to provide meals to Eastern Air Lines. Soon Hot Shoppes were appearing in airports across the country, and in 1957 the first Marriott Hotel opened in Arlington, Virginia.

Admittedly, dreaming of realizing success as great as that of a Hilton or Marriott may be a bit overwhelming. So let's take a look at a smaller operation that nevertheless has achieved a good deal of success.

Ferncroft Inn

Terry and Ade Nitschelm realized their dream by opening Ferncroft, an inn in New Hampshire's White Mountains.

Ade discovered the beauties of New Hampshire while attending Dartmouth College. He worked in Newark after graduation, but quickly decided that he wanted to return to the mountains. His dream was to operate a small inn where guests would feel at home the minute they stepped inside. Fortunately, he had no difficulty persuading Terry to share his dream.

Ade quit his job and worked in hotels for more than a year to gain experience. During this time Terry came into a small inheritance, and that, combined with a loan from a relative, allowed them to buy Pleasant Valley Farm, a run-down boarding house in Glen, New Hampshire.

The couple worked eighteen-hour days for a month converting the drab old house into a bright, modern inn. They worked hard, cleaning, scraping, painting, and wallpapering. Terry says that when the first guests arrived, she had literally just made their bed.

The Nitschelms relied on contributions from their families to help furnish the ten guest rooms and two living rooms. Rugs, furniture, books, and knickknacks were graciously donated by relatives for use at the inn. The items included lovely Oriental rugs and a valuable music box.

Ade explains that for several years he and Terry had to put every bit of money they earned back into the inn. Although it seemed that there wasn't enough room for the number of guests who wanted reservations, renovating additional rooms and building a cottage used all their cash. The beginning of every season found the couple broke because all of their earnings had gone into improving the facilities.

Terry and Ade wanted to expand on their dream by purchasing the former Bigelow mansion in nearby Intervale. Located in a grove of lofty pines and commanding a breathtaking view of the Presidential Range, this imposing and luxurious house contained ample bedrooms and baths for their growing business. Although the mansion had been closed for some time, it was in very good condition and the owner was anxious to sell. The Nitschelms bought the property and began another renovation project. Once they were able to open, returning guests found the new accommodations just as good as the original ones. The new Ferncroft can accommodate sixty guests.

Ade is responsible for meal planning, purchasing, and kitchen operation. He also handles maintenance of the inn, cottages, gift shop, and grounds. Terry supervises the guest rooms, the dining room, and all of the front-of-the-house activities, while raising four children.

Although the couple could continue to expand their property, they feel that doing so would take away from the inn's individuality and would adversely affect their relationships with returning guests. They strive to give guests the best in hospitality, including the very best available dining and sleeping options.

Ade and Terry attribute a big part of their success to the fact that they were able to put their profits back into the business, which has allowed them to continually improve the property. They feel that the story of their success can inspire other would-be innkeepers who have little to start with to work hard at achieving their dreams.

As Ade says, "Every reader of that book you're writing can dream as Terry and I have dreamed, and with a little cash, luck, and lots of honest-to-goodness hard work, they, too, can succeed."

Sweet Dreams and Toast

The bed-and-breakfast is a very popular type of accommodation. Many travelers prefer the cozy hospitality offered by a B and B over the anonymity of a large hotel. So rather than running her own bed-and-breakfast, Eleanor Chastain of Washington, DC, opened Sweet Dreams and Toast. Her company represents about a hundred homes that operate as B and Bs in Washington and Annapolis, Maryland. She charges a 20 percent commission to handle the reservations and collect guest charges in advance.

Experience Is the Best Teacher

If you are serious about opening a hospitality service business, one of the most important things you can do in preparation is to obtain experience in both the housekeeping and food service ends of the business. Without solid knowledge of the business, you simply can't succeed.

You need to understand how to order food and other supplies, how to plan and prepare menus, and how to supervise staff. Where will you advertise? If you are in a seasonally popular area, how will you earn money during the off-season? Even though your guests look to you for a wonderful vacation experience, you might find that you get little if any time off for yourself. You have to be completely comfortable with the accounting and bookkeeping requirements of running an inn, even if you hire an accountant. These are just a few of the items you need to consider very carefully before making an investment in this type of business.

However, if you enjoy meeting people, catering to their needs, and serving them, this can be a most satisfying business. Be prepared, though, to work hard and labor long hours, earn less than you are worth, and at a moment's notice take over any job in the house. In spite of the disadvantages, if you have hoteling in your blood, this could possibly be your life's work.

You can obtain more information about the hospitality industry in North America from the American Hotel and Lodging Association at www.ahla.com, or the Professional Association of Innkeepers International at www.paii.org.

Running an Airline

Major airlines aren't the only options for anyone interested in providing flight service. Airplane charters are one possibility, but you'll need to do a lot of market research to be successful in this already very crowded field. Another option, however, is a "flight-seeing" service that takes customers over interesting areas that command a spectacular aerial view.

Air Grand Canyon is a successful flight tour company that has operated out of Grand Canyon Airport in Prescott, Arizona, since 1981. The company was started by Dan and Cecily Lawler with one Cessna aircraft.

If you are an airplane buff eager to have a business of your own but can't see how to manage it, you'll be encouraged by the Lawlers' story of how they got their business up and running, despite some false starts and nearly losing everything along the way.

Dan Lawler is a model airplane enthusiast and a real aviation bug who had spent considerable time flying during his college years. "What does a college graduate do with a psychology background and a tremendous desire to get into aviation?" he asked. At that time, the general aviation field offered no opportunities for someone who knew how to fly, could instruct others, and could also do odd jobs around an airport. So Dan found one job collecting bills for a finance company and then another adjusting insurance claims. He spent weekends as a flight instructor in the Phoenix area and eventually found a job with a company that had government contracts to fight forest fires and do crop dusting. He got the chance to fly larger planes, even some old World War II reconditioned B-17 bombers. He also managed to keep up with his flight instructing and pilot certification work.

Dan still wanted to do more than offer flight instruction, so he started his own business providing scenic flights over the Grand Canyon. There was already a similar operator at the Grand Canyon Airport, which, under Arizona law at that time, precluded Dan from working there. He found a site to lease in Ashfork and used his limited savings to build a single dirt runway and lease a plane. Unfortunately, the business was too small for him to earn enough money, and a flood washed out his airstrip, leaving him with nothing.

Dan felt that his only choice was to return to Prescott and resume flight instruction. That was when he met Cecily, who was working as a bookkeeper.

He soon found a nearby airport where an operator had been offering scenic flights since 1946. Since the airport had received some federal aid for improvements, the owner could no longer maintain his monopoly, which made room for Dan. Although federal regulations clearly opened the airport to all qualified operators, it nevertheless took a good deal of negotiation and politicking before Dan received permission to start his flight service. Soon after, a third operator opened a service at the airport, which created a great deal of competition for a limited market.

Dan worked as the pilot for the tour service and Cecily kept the books, sold tickets, ran the office, and answered questions. They spent the summer living at the airport in a travel trailer and by fall had to admit that there wasn't enough business for three operators in the same field. The Lawlers and the third operator pulled out, leaving the original company once again the sole operator in the area.

Although they were discouraged, Dan and Cecily weren't ready to give up. Their lucky break came from a State Aeronautics Department official Dan knew. The official had had a disagreement with the sole operator at Grand Canyon Airport and was anxious to bring in some competition for that company. Since the airport is owned and operated by the State of Arizona, Dan was able to get in with his friend's encouragement.

Dan and Cecily leased a plane and ticket-counter space in the main terminal building and began to advertise their service. Although business that first winter was slow, the Lawlers were able to move from the trailer into a mobile home. Cecily greatly enjoyed working in the busy terminal, and Dan was again piloting the tours. Once spring arrived, the crowds returned to the area and business picked up considerably.

Dan mentions the importance of leasing planes for someone starting out in this type of business. He points out that many wealthy people own small planes that they like to lease for income as well as for tax advantages. You should inquire at a general aviation airport, where such planes would be stored or parked. Dan says that without the option of leasing, he and Cecily would never have been able to get their business going.

Air Grand Canyon has seen a steady rise in business since its somewhat uncertain beginning. The company started with Dan, Cecily, and a single Cessna. Today it has a fleet of twelve airplanes and a staff of twenty employees. Dan rarely flies, unless he needs to cover for a pilot who can't work. The company offers four tours, which range from an hour-long aerial tour of the Grand Canyon to a full-day tour that includes a river rafting trip down the Colorado River.

In summary, Dan Lawler says, "It's been hard work, heartbreak at times, but we kept at it. When we came to town nobody knew us, but little by little you get ahead. People hear about you. If you offer good service and play it honest, they will say good things about you and your service."

Travel Agency Services

Running a travel agency can be a wonderful way to provide a service to the public. So many people love to travel, and it can be very rewarding to help them plan that special trip. Even though the Internet has made it easy for passengers to book their own flights and accommodations, the sheer volume of information available on the Web combined with constantly changing airfares and schedules send many people to their local travel agent for assistance.

You don't necessarily need a college degree to work as a travel agent, but as in any business, it's a good idea to get some experience before going out on your own. Most established agencies prefer to hire new employees with some education beyond high school. Many vocational schools offer full-time travel agent programs that last several months, as well as evening and weekend programs. Travel agent courses are also offered in public adult education programs and in community and four-year colleges. A few colleges offer bachelor's or master's degrees in travel and tourism. In addition to training, any personal travel experience or experience as an airline reservation agent is an asset, because your knowledge about a city or foreign country can help influence a client's travel plans.

You'll need a few personal qualities to succeed as a travel agent. You must be well organized, accurate, and meticulous to compile information from several sources and plan a client's itinerary. You should also be patient—many clients change their minds about their travel plans, and sometimes finding what a client wants can take a good deal of research. If you plan to specialize in business travel, be prepared to work very quickly because business travel plans often change on short notice.

Before you can start earning commissions in your own agency, you must gain formal approval from suppliers and corporations such as airlines, ship lines, or rail lines. For example, the Airlines Reporting Corporation and the International Airlines Travel Agency Network are the approving bodies for airlines. To gain their approval, an agency must be financially sound and employ at least one experienced manager or agent.

For information about all aspects of the travel agency industry in the United States and Canada, contact the American Association of Travel Agents at www.astanet.com.

A Final Word

After reading this chapter you can see that travel provides more opportunities for service businesses than you might have expected.

Providing accommodations, operating a means of transportation, and coordinating travel itineraries are but a few of the possibilities in this wide-open field. If you think carefully about the many aspects of travel and do some reading on the subject, you just might come up with an innovative service that travelers would be happy to pay for.

11

WHO CAN FIX IT?

WHO DO YOU call when your oven doesn't work? Where do you turn when another driver hits your car and dents the fender? What about when your computer crashes? In each of these cases, and in many others, you call on a service technician or repairperson.

Everyone owns something that will eventually need to be repaired, whether it's a car, a plasma television, or a leaky roof. If you have the interest, ability, and skills, you can develop a service business in one of many areas of service and repair. Depending on the particular service you choose to offer, you might find training at trade and vocational schools, or you may get some on-the-job experience by working for a similar business. You can also find books that provide useful information about repairs and services.

General information about careers and a directory of accredited trade and technical schools are available from the Accrediting Commission of Career Schools and Colleges of Technology. Visit www.accsct.org for details.

For an idea of the broad range of repair services that exist, look in the yellow pages under "Repair Service—General." You'll find such categories as "*See* Appliances—Small—Repairs and Service"; "Automobile Repairing and Servicing"; "Cameras—Repairing"; "Furniture Repairing and Refinishing"; "Jewelry—Repairing"; "Oil Burners—Servicing"; and "Spas and Hot Tubs—Repairs and Service." This does not include the large category of home repairs performed by such crafts workers as carpenters, electricians, painters, plumbers, and roofers.

Most repair services don't require much capital. You may have to rent space for a business such as an auto repair shop, but you can repair appliances or run a carpentry business out of your home. In the latter case, you'll need a reliable vehicle for traveling to jobs and carrying equipment.

You've probably heard people complain about repair services, and chances are you've had your own experience waiting eight hours for a service technician or being dissatisfied with the work once it's finally done. It's unfortunately true that many people who don't have the right skills or temperament for this business nevertheless see it as a way to make a lot of money without caring much about their reputations. That's why you will have a great advantage if you start a competing business of your own. Offer a superior service at fair rates, and you should have no trouble establishing yourself as the number one service in your community. That is what Bob Wood has done as a house painter in Boulder, Colorado.

Profitable Paintbrush

From Bob Wood's observation, Boulder has something in common with most other large prosperous areas—the greater the average income of residents, the fewer who want to do inside and outside painting themselves.

Before entering this occupation, Bob was a professional drummer playing with a well-known band, but he tired of the endless travel. He wanted something that would be steady, pay well, and, if at all possible, enable him to work outdoors during good weather. A friend in Connecticut, who was a painting contractor and who also happened to have an overloaded schedule, asked if Bob could lend a hand. Bob reluctantly said yes, but then he discovered he enjoyed the work.

Although the affluent Connecticut county seemed to have more jobs than painters to do them, Bob was more interested in moving west. On a trip to Colorado, he became enamored of Boulder, with its mountains and winter sports and plenty of opportunity for someone with his skills. He joined a small firm and since then has had trouble finding enough time away from the job to enjoy the benefits of living in the Rockies.

Bob describes a painting company as an ideal occupation for a young person who wants to start a business, and he feels the same way about services in plumbing, carpentry, roof repair, or any other craft service.

The main thing you'll need to get started is a vehicle, preferably a light pickup truck. It doesn't have to be brand new, but it must have the capacity to carry ladders along with all the other supplies a painter needs.

Bob prefers to use a light ladder, which is an extension-type ladder that extends to eighteen feet long. A stepladder is also a must, as well as quality brushes of varying widths. He suggests asking a professional at a good hardware store or home center for help in selecting the right items. And speaking of ladders, he cautions that if you aren't comfortable climbing them or are afraid of heights, it might be a good idea to reconsider your business choice.

Bob also stresses the importance of maintaining a neat appearance. "Neat coveralls are an important item, too, and you need several pairs so you can have a clean one handy," Bob says. "Let me tell you that nothing inspires confidence in the customer as much as a neat painter. Sure you get paint on the coverall, but it doesn't have to be grimy."

An enterprising painter can work even when the weather seems to be against him. Bob explained that while he can't paint a damp surface, he can always find other tasks such as scraping and sanding, or preparing wood for painting once it's dry. He also generally has a backlog of indoor work on either residential or commercial projects. Bob naturally prefers to do all the outside work during the warmer weather, but he has learned to be flexible and juggle his jobs so that he can always stay busy.

Bob is glad that he chose to work for a company before starting his own business.

"I guess you might say that almost every painter's goal is to be his own boss, so why not me?" he asks. "But it doesn't hurt a bit to get experience in this business working for someone else before you launch your own company."

Keeping the Heat On

In some ways it seems that Ed Jarvis's choice of a service occupation was almost inevitable. While in high school he became interested in Vocational Industrial Clubs of America (VICA) and was elected vice president of the state organization in his junior year. He traveled to Oklahoma City and Washington, DC, for conventions and learned a lot about business. Early in his senior year he grew tired of school and decided to drop out. When two of the vocational teachers learned about his decision, they called him to their office.

"They backed me into a corner," Ed recalled, "and they really gave it to me. They pointed out that it would be idiotic to quit now, that I had an obligation to continue my membership in VICA, and that to drop out would be a disservice to myself and the school. In fact, they got me so mad that I jumped up and said, 'I'll stick it out! Just you wait and see what I can do!'"

Ed did just that. At the next state convention he was not only elected president but also won five awards, the first member ever to take all of the top honors in the same year. This recognition, plus being named a National Honor Student, qualified him to become the school's first student advisor to other students.

During this time, Ed worked every day from 7:30 A.M. until noon as an electrician's apprentice for a local company and attended classes in the afternoon. Once a week he studied electrical theory and practice at night school, and on other evenings he could be found working with the vocational teachers to convince town voters that they should approve funds for a vocational training school. The proposition passed, and Ed had the honor of taking part in the ground-breaking ceremony.

When graduation came he was offered an all-expenses-paid college education, but he turned it down. He says, "I was sick of school, and I had a job doing what I wanted to do. Even though the generous offer would not have to be repaid, I would always feel obligated to do that, and I didn't want to saddle myself with such a large debt. Anyway, I knew what I wanted to do, so why go to college?"

He took a higher-paying job with another electrician's company and worked until his area was hit by a recession. Ed was laid off twice, once when his wife was pregnant and again when they had two children.

Since his job with the electrician primarily involved working on new construction, Ed decided to look for year-round employment to avoid the slowdowns caused by cold weather. He found what he was looking for in the service department of an oil company. In this new job, he made service calls all winter and service and installation calls during the rest of the year. Training consisted of observing another serviceman for two weeks, after which he received his tools, truck, and a list of burners to be serviced.

Ed found that his associates were not eager to share their knowledge with a new employee, for fear he might get ahead of them. Then the company sent him for a week's training at a special technical school near Boston. He spent half his time in classes and the rest of the day with his instructor, who acted as a tutor. He made the most of this opportunity to learn as much as possible.

Back on the job, tension increased and Ed became frustrated and unhappy with some management decisions. Many customers had service contracts that entitled them to an annual cleaning and check plus free service calls if the burner stopped operating. The company felt that the cleaning and check should be limited to changing the oil filter, quickly cleaning things with a chemical solvent, and then moving on to the next job. Ed disagreed, believing it was necessary to pull out the front of the unit, inspect it, and clean it, which took more time than the company allowed for these calls.

The tension caused by this difference of opinion led Ed's wife to encourage him to start his own business. Intrigued by the idea, he approached another member of the service staff about forming a partnership. The men agreed to wait six months and then resign and start their own company. Unfortunately, the other employee told the boss about Ed's plan. The boss confronted Ed about the situation, which only led to more workplace tension.

Undaunted, Ed spoke with a friend who was a loan officer at a bank and was approved for a loan to buy a truck, tools, testing instruments, and other equipment. He gave two weeks' notice the next day, and as soon as he left the job, he began calling on prospective customers and shopping for a truck and equipment. He was certainly worried about the future, but two weeks later he was servicing an oil burner on his first job and had enough work lined up to keep him busy for three weeks.

Ed credits his wife with much of his success. Her constant encouragement and belief in his ability gave him the courage to strike out on his own. She still helps out by answering the phone and handling the billing for the company.

Ed hopes to expand the business, eventually having a crew of seven service technicians and as many trucks. He has been approached by a local oil company that wants him to take over all of its accounts, which would add three hundred to his existing twelve hundred clients. He plans to train new employees himself, instructing them in the basics of cleaning and testing a burner and furnace, replacing parts, and doing minor repairs. The biggest jobs involve a burner that won't start or that malfunctions for no apparent reason. These situations are when Ed's years of experience make the difference, because he believes in fixing a problem on the first service call.

Of course, adding more employees means more expenses, such as salary, Social Security contributions, unemployment tax, insurance, and tools and equipment. But Ed is confident that he can secure additional financing from his bank to cover the increased expenses.

One thing Ed won't do is sacrifice family time for the business. He will work only five days a week, saving weekends for his wife and children.

If, like Ed Jarvis, your goal is to give good service, provide adequately for your family, and still have time for your spouse and children, you, too, could achieve success in your chosen field, as he has in his. When a service is needed in the community and you work consistently to supply it, your chances at success are very good.

Appliance Repair Service

Good appliance repair services are also in demand. Randy Fairfax found this to be true in a St. Louis suburb. He started a repair service that concentrates on washing machines, dryers, dishwashers, refrigerators, and freezers. (Small appliances are usually returned to the factory for repairs or to an authorized repair center.)

His only competition initially came from the retail stores that sold the appliances and provided service under a warranty. But the service was difficult to obtain from some retailers, and after the warranty on a product had expired, customers might wait days or weeks for someone to come and fix the problem.

Randy works out of his home, and his wife handles the telephone and makes appointments for him. He doesn't have to carry a large parts inventory because he keeps a stock of secondhand or reconditioned parts that he can use to get a machine operating while he orders a new part from the manufacturer. This ensures immediate repairs and customer satisfaction and also keeps his overhead down.

He also makes it a practice to let customers know if he is going to be late or unable to come. "It's somewhat like a doctor's office," he says. "A repair may take longer than you thought, and that throws our whole schedule into chaos for the day or the week. It's only fair to let people know if you cannot keep your appointment. That's something that many of the other service people neglect to do."

Randy advertises in the yellow pages, choosing a simple and inexpensive listing that he finds well worth the cost.

What we have discovered here about painting and furnace and appliance repair services applies also to other crafts. Carpenters, plumbers, roofers, electricians, chimney cleaners and repairers, masons, as well as jewelers, shoe repairers, tailors, radio/TV repairers, and others have many features in common. In many communities it is difficult to find someone who can provide prompt and reliable service. There is every indication that that need will continue indefinitely.

Transmissions by Lucille

Men aren't the only ones who can build successful service careers. Women are entering this repair area in ever-increasing numbers.

Lucille Treganowan, of Pittsburgh, had to find a job when it became necessary for her to support her three children. She was hired to do clerical work in the service department of a transmission repair shop, where she filled orders for parts and answered questions about transmissions. Although she knew nothing about transmissions when she started the job, Lucille was soon so expert that she was advising the mechanics and ultimately became a third partner in the business.

Four years later she decided to start her own business, obtained a $25,000 loan from the Small Business Administration, and rented a vacant gas station. The SBA loan plus $5,000 of personal savings enabled her to buy the necessary tools, machines, and parts to open her transmission repair shop. A transmission repair shop was such a novelty that the media gave Lucille free advertising, and her business was a hit.

Eighteen months later, with a $130,000 bank loan, Lucille purchased a former used-car showroom. Here she was able to have all of the work done out in the open, where customers could see the mechanics in action. It was a bright, clean repair shop, and in a short time Lucille opened another branch, using her profits for the expansion.

Before long she became a celebrity, hosting her own television show about auto repair on HGTV, teaching classes, and publishing a book titled *Lucille's Car Care: Everything You Need to Know from Under the Hood—By America's Most Trusted Mechanic.* She was profiled in the *New York Times* and has appeared on "The Today Show," "Dateline NBC," "Oprah," and the popular sitcom "Home Improvement."

A Final Word

There are so many opportunities in repair service businesses that it's impossible to list them all. From automobiles to computers to appliances, these are just a few of the areas in which people regularly need repair service. With a little imagination, an honest assessment of your skills, and an ability to learn, you can create a successful career in one of these interesting areas.

12

THE CUSTOMER'S HOME

YOU MIGHT FIND inspiration for a service business right in your own neighborhood. Think about the population of your town, and consider residents who may have special needs you could provide, such as babysitting, house-sitting, cleaning, lawn mowing, landscaping, trash collecting, pet-sitting, shopping, chauffeuring, painting, wallpapering, carpentry, or house repair services, to name just a few. Some services, such as caring for children, attending to shut-ins or the sick, cooking for a family, and tutoring are all positions that call for some training, which you can generally obtain from local adult-education classes or community college courses.

Some services, such as cooking or caring for an elderly resident, will be on a one-to-one basis, where you work on a daily schedule for that employer. Other services, such as lawn care, painting, or house cleaning, are examples of businesses you would offer to many people, and you would line up regular customers to keep you busy.

Most of these services call for little, if any, financial investment on your part, except those for any tools or equipment that you'll need to complete the job, such as a lawn mower, cleaning equipment, or garden tools. At first you may be able to borrow or rent these and wait until your business is firmly established before investing in your own.

Caring for homes is a growing multimillion-dollar industry. Residents seek services that provide security, functionality, cleanliness, and beauty. The market for these services is nationwide, except in low-income rural and urban areas.

Home Electronics

It's difficult to find a home today that doesn't have several pieces of electronic equipment, such as televisions, stereos, CD and DVD players, and video cameras. An increasing number of homes also have electronic security systems, intercom equipment, satellite television dishes, and home-theater systems.

While many of us like having the most current electronics in our homes, very few of us would be able to repair any of it if it stopped working. The technology is so advanced that most of us can't even install the equipment on our own and often need lessons in how to work the various components of these sophisticated systems. This means that most people need to hire someone to help them both operate and repair their electronic systems.

If you have basic knowledge and skills in electronics and familiarity with reading schematics, you may be able to build a business in this growing area. Vocational programs and community colleges offer training programs that include both hands-on experience and theoretical education in digital consumer electronics.

Once you've got some training, you can apply for a job with an established installation and repair service. As a new employee, you'll most likely start by working closely with a more experienced technician until you are ready to go out on your own. As you gain more experience, you may decide to specialize in a particular area of electronics or become a troubleshooter who can diagnose difficult problems. You may even become certified by manufacturers in the installation and repair of their particular equipment.

Once you start your own installation and repair business, you'll need a vehicle to get to appointments and an answering machine or voice-mail system so you don't miss any calls from customers. Remember that you'll be working in customers' homes, often teaching them how to use equipment that baffles them, so you'll need to be patient and able to make a point clearly. Customers will be happy to recommend someone who made all the technical jargon sound simple and who made that fancy new home-theater system actually work.

Home Security

People who own paintings, silver, antiques, and other valuables often find that insuring their homes can be quite expensive without the discount that insurance companies allow for the use of electronic burglar alarm systems. And more and more average home owners who simply want the most protection for their families are installing security systems. Some of these systems are connected directly to an alarm at the nearest police headquarters; others are wired to private alarm centers that can receive signals indicating burglary, fire, frozen pipes, robbery, or medical emergency, depending on which services the subscriber chooses.

One option in home security services is a business that installs and monitors alarm systems. Some businesses specialize in home security systems, providing round-the-clock monitoring service for subscribers.

If you like the idea of a home security business but don't have the necessary training in electronics, there is another protective service that relies completely on people and is inexpensive to organize. A house-sitting business with a market among households that do not have expensive electronic surveillance systems provides an opportunity in another area of home security.

House-Sitting Security Service

Like many city dwellers, residents in Tucson, Arizona, are concerned about home security, which makes a house-sitting service a great opportunity. Jane Poston saw the opportunity and created an extremely successful service that caters to people who need sitters to watch homes, water plants, care for pets, pick up mail, and give home owners a sense of security while they are away.

Jane has had a varied career. She worked in Boston for a textbook publisher and also wrote and recorded scripts for a series of thirty ten-minute programs on yoga. She taught English at Palo Verde High School, later at Pima Community College, and next joined the Peace Corps. She is currently spokeswoman for the city of Chandler, Arizona.

When Jane returned to Tucson after working for the Peace Corps, she found that there were no openings for English teachers in the school system and decided to start her own business. To gain exposure, she persuaded the local newspaper to print a feature story on her new enterprise. Jane staffed her company with fifteen retirees who were willing to move into a client's home and be on hand in the event of an emergency, such as a leaky pipe or power failure.

Retired people are ideal for this work because they often prefer to stay home and have had a lifetime of experience caring for their own homes. As a prerequisite, the people Jane hires must own or rent homes in Tucson, and she personally screens each applicant and obtains three character references before hiring anyone.

Jane believes this is a valuable service both to the elderly and all home owners who need this protection. She tries to match each home to the sitter and respects the client's preference for a couple or a single man or woman. She splits her fee with the house-sitter.

Jane says that a home-sitting service business can be set up for minimal expense, can be full- or part-time, and doesn't require expensive training. Her self-published guide, *How to Run a House-Sitting Business*, provides everything you need to know about starting and operating such an enterprise.

Home Cleaning

Another priority for home owners and renters is keeping their homes clean. This can be an especially lucrative service business given the fact that in so many households, both spouses or partners work full-time. Also, many women who work from home would rather spend more time with their children than clean.

This area has lots of potential for a service business career. Read the following account of a Midwestern organization that serves both businesses and residential customers through a clever, thoroughly workable system. This firm has laid out a sure blueprint for success.

Building and Maintenance Service

One of the oldest, largest, and most comprehensive building maintenance services in the Midwest is the Des Moines firm Building Maintenance Service (BMS*), founded by Dale V. Nelson. In case you are wondering about the asterisk, it's part of the company's registered trademark and stands for "the sign of quality."

Dale Nelson was the son of a dairy farmer. He moved to Iowa to work as a salesman for a floor-care products manufacturer and during his travels realized that most commercial cleaning services were nothing more than small, informal janitorial operations. Believing that the business had great potential and that he could do a much more professional job than was then available, he founded Building Maintenance Service. Dale advertised that his company was ready to clean offices, shopping malls, warehouses, and all types of commercial buildings. From that start as a one-man organization, his company grew over the next ten years to employ some five hundred people with record annual sales of over $4 million.

What makes this business so interesting is its broad line of services: full twenty-four-hour custodial services, twenty-four-hour emergency service, carpet cleaning, upholstery and other furniture cleaning, drapery cleaning, carpeting and floor covering repair, snow removal, full lawn-care service, window cleaning, ceiling cleaning, parking lot sweeping, painting and wall patching, and even full-time industrial engineering.

In addition, Dale diversified by opening two other companies under his corporate umbrella:

• CIC Plan, Inc., a national cash-collection agency of bad debts for a variety of clients such as major credit card centers, airlines, national banks, and other companies, hospitals, and physicians
• The more recently organized Maid in Des Moines, a professional maid service aimed at the residential market

Maid in Des Moines

Kent Knudson, president of Maid in Des Moines, developed his business concept when he noticed that many cleaning services were run by husband-and-wife teams who, for the most part, were unable to make a success of their businesses. He saw a profitable niche for the service if developed and marketed properly. Dale Nelson was the person who helped make it happen by giving Kent both encouragement and affiliation with his own company.

Initially Kent, the president, was the only full-time worker, with two part-time assistants. He found his first customers through word-of-mouth recommendations, and soon he had monthly contracts with a dozen clients.

The company offers services on a weekly, biweekly, or monthly basis: completely sanitized bathrooms and kitchens; vacuumed and edged carpeting; vacuumed upholstered furniture; mopped and refinished floors; dusted and polished furniture, ledges, and sills; cleaned and sanitized appliance surfaces; removed cobwebs.

Custom cleaning is available on request and includes cleaning before and/or after parties, special occasions, and relocating/moving; cleaning carpets, upholstery, windows, and appliances; polishing silver, chandeliers, and light fixtures; and cleaning out garages and basements. Custom cleaning also includes cleaning attics, washing dishes, and even making beds.

Cleaning is cleverly systemized; the professionals start in the corners of each room and clean inward. All surfaces are cleared so that they can be cleaned and then the items replaced. When asked how they remember where to replace the things they remove from tables, dressers, and counters, Kent says, "Putting things back is the habit of a professional cleaner."

Home Decor

Home owners want to maintain a beautiful environment, both inside and out. For the interior of the home, decorating services help plan the decor and can even take care of all the necessary details to achieve a beautiful result. To succeed in this business, you must have a feeling for interior decorating, a sense of color, and an almost instinctive ability to pull together all the elements needed to create a lovely room and to make that room a part of an integrated house interior. There are books on interior decorating; and there may be formal courses given in your area. As in other fields, your best plan is to study and work for an interior decorator to gain practical experience before you strike out on your own.

Landscape and Gardening Service

Landscape gardening is one of the most important occupations concerned with improving our environment and maintaining an attractive home. What the forester is to the care and preservation of woodlands, the gardener is to the maintenance and improvement of residential and commercial gardens, as well as parks and other open space in cities.

Michael Rush is a successful landscape gardener from Prescott, Arizona. After he graduated from high school in Cincinnati, he fell in love with the West, attracted by its open spaces, beauty, and friendly residents. Uncertain of what to do for a living, he took a job as a handyman at a factory. Then Michael learned of an opening with the USDA Forest Service, working as a forester in the Prescott National Forest. He was assigned to a project landscaping one of the building compounds, and he quickly discovered that he enjoyed working outdoors as well as learning about trees, plants, bushes, and other growing things.

Since the work was seasonal, Michael decided to look for a landscaping job that would provide year-round employment. He inquired at city hall and learned of an opening for a gardener.

For the next three years Michael worked hard and learned all he could, doing maintenance work during the growing season and landscaping in the off-season. While working in this capacity he met Bob Swope, who had started a small yard and lawn service. Bob had residential and commercial customers for cutting lawns, clipping, pruning, weeding, cleaning out beds, and planting. He operated the business himself and would ask Michael to help out when he found it difficult to keep up with his schedule.

When Bob decided to move away from Arizona, he sold the business to Michael. "Once we had completed the deal," Michael says, "I realized that I had a truck, gardening equipment for one man, and twelve accounts. That, I knew, would never support a family, so I went to work. I worked alone that first year, then as business grew by 25 percent each year, I added to my staff. Now I am servicing some sixty accounts and also doing all of the city's maintenance work on a year-round contractual basis."

Michael has five employees. During the growing season the entire staff works five days a week, and during the off-season three work full-time and the others are part-time. He owns three pick-up trucks and a larger truck to haul debris to the dump or carry shrubs, trees, and other materials, in addition to an extensive inventory of shovels, rakes, hoes, lawn mowers, and other equipment.

When asked about the competition, Michael says that although there are four or five other lawn services in the area, each has its own regular customers, so they don't take business away from one another.

The services that Michael offers include lawn mowing and trimming; tree and shrub pruning; design, planting, and care of flower beds; weed and insect control; fertilizing; landscape construction; and greenhouse management (propagation of flowers for beds). In addition, he must supervise his crews, prepare job estimates, promote the business, and plan for projected growth and his equipment and manpower needs.

Michael keeps his books, which he finds a chore, although he admits it is rewarding, too. "I really enjoy being in business for myself," he says. "I work long hours some weeks, but there's satisfaction in knowing that it's your own service and that you are responsible for keeping the grounds of so many homes and businesses well groomed and attractive. It takes a certain type of person to run a business. I have to keep a tight schedule and discipline myself."

Michael admits that sometimes business does interfere with his family life, particularly during the busy season when he works longer hours, but he does his best to maintain a healthy balance between work and home. It helps that his wife gets involved in the business by giving him a hand with the bookkeeping and making valuable suggestions about landscaping projects.

A Final Word

People take great pride in their homes, so they look for professionals who can provide high-quality services that they will be happy to live with for years to come. If you are skilled at home improvement and repair work or have the creative ability to decorate a home inside or out, you may be on your way to success in a home-related service business.

13

Services for Individuals

You've already seen that there are many different types of service businesses. Some involve services targeted at a group of people, while others give you an opportunity to work with individuals.

Most of the businesses described in this chapter involve working in a one-on-one relationship with a person who requires your service. The story of Wally Amos is included here because it is unusual in that it illustrates how a career in a service operation can switch to an entirely different area, in this case a successful cookie business—Famous Amos Cookies.

There is great variety in the types of personal services, ranging from insurance counseling and hairstyling to consulting as a tax expert to serving as a theatrical agent. One thing all these services have in common is that they serve individuals and in some way help make their lives more pleasant, easier, or more secure. There is no easy way to classify these services or any logical order in which to present them. Therefore, let's start with a very familiar personal service business—the hair salon.

Hair Salons

Auto repair, home maintenance, and food services are all essential industries that are for the most part recession-proof. The same is generally true for hairstylists or beauticians. Whether there is depression or prosperity, one thing is certain—people want to look their best and will seek the services of skilled cosmetologists. Holiday Hair Fashions, a company that survived the recession of the 1980s and continues to maintain stores throughout Pennsylvania, more than proves this point. If you are interested in starting your own hairstyling service, you will be encouraged by the accomplishments of Raymond E. Holland, president of this rapidly expanding company.

Raymond grew up during the 1930s on a tobacco farm in rural North Carolina in a house without electricity. When Ray was a teenager, his father sold the family farm to purchase a country store, where Raymond received his first business experience waiting on customers and lugging cases of canned foods up from the cellar.

When he graduated from high school, Ray found a job as a helper in a nearby air-conditioning firm. He was making $1.10 an hour, so he decided there was no future in the firm and drove north to seek his fortune. He took a number of short-term jobs in Pennsylvania's Lehigh Valley but soon realized that he needed to find permanent work.

On the advice of a relative, he entered a local beauty school and, at age twenty-two, completed his training and found work in a small shop. He later made several changes in the shop to improve service and the store's profits.

Ray invested his life savings of $1,400 to lease a store and obtain the necessary equipment for his hairstyling business. He opened his service to the public on a Labor Day. From the beginning it was a success, thanks to his outgoing personality, his knowledge of the business, and his natural talent in marketing and promotion.

In time he opened a second store, then a third, and eventually the chain included forty stores. (He prefers to call them stores rather than shops.) The next step in his expansion program was to locate the stores in places such as malls and shopping centers with high consumer traffic and adequate parking. He knew these sites would help build both sales volume and profits.

Ray became president of the newly incorporated company with headquarters in Allentown, Pennsylvania. Five years later, Holiday Hair Fashions was employing twelve hundred people in eight states and opening an average of two new stores every month. More astounding is the fact that its employees were cutting or styling hair for some thirty thousand customers a week.

Ray identifies three specific points that led to the success of his chain of stores. As you can see, Ray insists on making the service convenient to the customer.

- The stores accept "walk-ins," customers who do not have appointments, which can be especially profitable in a busy mall or shopping center.
- The stores are open daily from 8:00 A.M. to 8:00 P.M.
- Prices are kept at reasonable levels.

Other factors have contributed to the success of the operation. The company promotes its employees from within its ranks and offers excellent working conditions, profit sharing, and bonuses. A monthly newsletter keeps employees informed about the company and about employees' activities and personal achievements—and the top bonus earners.

When not managing the business, inspecting the many stores, or attending employee functions, Ray keeps busy helping United Cerebral Palsy and other charities. He also pursues his hobby of collecting automobile art and pre-World War I antique toys. (*Motor Car in Art: Selections from the Raymond E. Holland Automotive Art Collection*, by John Zolomij, profiles Raymond's collection.)

For more information about barber and cosmetology schools, contact the American Association of Cosmetology Schools at www.beautyschools.org. Information about the industry in North America is available from the National Cosmetology Association at www.ncacares.org. For a list of licensed training schools and the licensing requirements for cosmetologists, contact the National Accrediting Commission of Cosmetology Arts and Sciences at www.naccas.org.

Independent Insurance Agent

The insurance industry provides many opportunities for service businesses. Just think about it—nearly everyone owns something that they insure. We buy policies for our homes, autos, businesses, and for our very lives. And for personal service and sound advice, we consult an insurance agent or broker.

To differentiate, an agent works for an insurance company; a broker is an independent agent who may sell policies for many different companies. Agents and brokers sell one or more of the three basic types of insurance: life, property-liability (casualty), and health. Many life and casualty agents also sell health insurance policies covering the costs of hospital and medical care or loss of income due to illness or injury. Some agents also advise clients about buying securities, such as shares in mutual funds or variable annuities.

This is one service field in which education and training are a necessity. You will need a college degree to work in insurance. Many colleges and universities offer courses in insurance, and a few schools offer a bachelor's degree in the field. Courses in finance, mathematics, accounting, economics, business law, marketing, and business administration will enable you to understand how social and economic conditions relate to the insurance industry. You will also need to be familiar with computers and software packages because these are widely used throughout the industry.

You will have to be licensed by the state or province in which you plan to work. In most localities, this involves completing specified prelicensing courses and passing the required exams that cover insurance fundamentals and state or provincial insurance laws.

As the demand for financial products and financial planning increases, many insurance agents are choosing to gain the proper licensing and certification to sell securities and other financial products. If you choose to do so, you will have to pass either the Series 6 or Series 7 licensing exam, which is administered by the National Association of Securities Dealers.

All forms of insurance provide protection against loss from disaster and offer peace of mind to the insured. The conscientious life insurance agent or broker finds great personal satisfaction in helping families plan for their financial security in the event something happens to a wage earner. This was what appealed to William Merton when he investigated the industry. His experience may encourage anyone who is interested in embarking on a life insurance career.

Providing Peace of Mind

William Merton was introduced to the insurance business by an agent who shared his philosophy of working in this service area. He saw the insurance agent as someone who had an understanding of human problems and an awareness of how the right insurance can help to offset them.

William specializes in life insurance and always tries to put himself in the place of his clients to better understand their needs. "Actually," he says, "I work for the families of my clients, rather than for those who sign the applications and draw the checks. I like to think of each member of a family as a face, not just a name."

For example, a client who was insured for $120,000 once asked to cancel half of his insurance policy to get the cash to cover a temporary business reversal. William persuaded the client that it would be a better idea to borrow the money than to surrender his policy and further convinced him to wait until he felt it was absolutely necessary to secure a loan. The client took William's advice. Two weeks later, the man died and his family was still protected by full coverage and didn't have to repay a loan.

William sees service, rather than immediate personal profit, as the basic criterion of his work. He considers himself a consultant, not a salesman, and selects his prospects carefully, attempting to approach only those who can afford and will benefit from the service he offers. Once having offered that service, he gives exactly the same attention to those who do not buy additional insurance as to those who do. This includes periodic reviews of their life insurance programs and adjustments whenever a birth or death, a new job, additional group or pension insurance, or changes in Social Security or tax laws occur.

This attitude has paid off handsomely indeed. In his second full year in the business, William led the agency in production by more than $400,000. And he managed to accomplish this despite the opinion of one advertising agency executive who said William would be certain to fail if he insisted on believing that "life insurance doesn't have to be sold."

William Merton's experience proves how right he was. Almost all of his business comes from old clients or from friends to whom they have recommended his services as a consultant. He acknowledges that he frequently works evenings, weekends, and holidays, but this doesn't bother him.

"I get a real kick out of my work," William says. "There's nothing like it for the man or woman who likes people and who wants to feel he or she is doing something worthwhile for them. There's no greater satisfaction than to know that your advice has brought peace of mind to your clients as well as financial security to their dependents."

As an independent agent or broker selling casualty or medical insurance, you can offer peace of mind to clients who are concerned about fire, theft, storms, accidents, sickness, and other hazards.

General information about insurance agents and brokers is available from the home offices of many insurance companies. Your state or provincial department of insurance can provide information about licensing requirements. You can obtain further information about starting an insurance business from the following sources: Insurance Information Institute at www.iii.org; Independent Insurance Agents and Brokers of America at www.iiaa.org; and Insurance Brokers Association of Canada at www.ibac.ca.

Tax Consultant

Many people dread taking care of their own taxes; they are afraid of making costly mistakes or simply intimidated by the complexity of tax forms and changing laws. Many turn to large companies that provide income tax preparation, but a great number of people still prefer to work with an individual who can make the process more personal. If you like math and interpreting government laws and regulations, preparing income tax returns may prove ideal for you. You don't have to be a certified public accountant to qualify for the work, although you should obtain some specialized training.

Wilhelmine Fuhrer of Auburn, Indiana, built a skyrocketing tax consulting business working from her home. She learned the fundamentals of preparing tax returns while working in the office of a lumber company. Her next job was with an insurance company, where she worked until her husband bought a farm. Unfortunately, farming was difficult and the couple went into debt. Realizing that extra income was a necessity but wanting to stay at home with her children, Wilhelmine drew on her experience and advertised in local newspapers as a tax return preparer.

She had twelve clients the first year and set a goal of doubling the number each year. She did just that but began to realize there was a limit to the number of returns she could handle alone. As her client roster grew, so did the stacks of tax forms and files, and she eventually put up a separate building on their property. The business continued to expand, and she soon had clients from eighteen states. This necessitated an addition to the original building.

Wilhelmine believes in giving her clients the best service and in taking the time to discuss their problems with them. In the course of her work she has encountered a variety of situations, ranging from clients who are overextended and need to be told what to do to pay off their debts to small businesses that have failed to keep proper accounts to dishonest individuals whose returns she refuses to sign.

If this field interests you, learn all you can about the subject. Take a course or two on tax accounting at a local community college or a school offering extension classes, and obtain experience working for one of the chains that prepare tax returns. They usually hire temporary employees during the busy spring season. Being a competent tax return consultant and preparer is a matter of knowing the subject; understanding how to read and interpret tax laws, regulations, and court decisions; and keeping up to date on current tax developments. There are excellent subscription tax services that give you the latest weekly developments.

Real Estate Agents and Brokers

More than a half million people work as real estate agents and brokers throughout North America. Although the real estate market has occasional downturns, this is generally a profitable service because our growing population will continue to increase demand for housing. As in the insurance industry, there is a difference between agents and brokers in real estate. Real estate agents usually are independent sales workers who provide their services to a licensed real estate broker on a contract basis. In return, the broker pays the agent a portion of the commission earned from the agent's sale of the property. Brokers are independent businesspeople who sell real estate owned by others; they also may rent or manage properties for a fee.

Although there might seem to be a proliferation of real estate agencies in most areas, this doesn't mean that there isn't room for your business. There is a relatively high turnover rate in this industry, so brokers are usually glad to welcome newcomers willing to risk investing their time in showing properties offered for sale.

All real estate brokers and agents must be licensed by the state or province where they work. The examinations, more comprehensive for brokers than for agents, include questions on basic real estate transactions and on laws affecting the sale of property. For information, contact the Real Estate Commission at your state or provincial capital.

Stewart Bacon sold real estate on weekends in Buffalo, New York, to supplement his salary as a teacher. After his death, his wife, Carol, took over the business briefly and then moved to Florida, arriving just in time to profit from a real estate boom. Thanks to her personality, drive, and keen desire to give the best possible service to all her clients—both buyers and sellers—she established a reputation as an enterprising and honest broker.

Carol says that one of the difficulties that brokers and agents face is that they represent both the buyer and seller of a property. Since each has a different objective, one to buy at the lowest cost, the other to sell at the highest price, it is up to the agent to find the right property for the buyer while making the best possible deal for the seller.

She went on to explain that most transactions work out easily, the prospective buyer making an offer that, if too low, is met by a counterproposal from the seller. The broker goes back and forth with offers as often as may be necessary until there is either agreement or the negotiations fall through.

"Occasionally I have a difficult client," Carol added. "Nothing suits; you spend days showing houses, often making offers that are unrealistic and wasting too much time. But you must be ready to do this if you are in this business. The stakes can be high and you should expect to work hard to earn each commission. If you are employed, it's a good business to try out on a part-time basis, as my husband did Saturdays and weekends. Then, if it works out and you like it, the next step is to work full-time and hustle!"

For further information, contact the National Association of Realtors at www.realtor.org or the Canadian Real Estate Association at www.crea.ca.

Child-Care Services

Like many people, Karrie Pomerantz earned extra money as a teenager by babysitting. She found that she enjoyed being with children and decided to study child psychology and early childhood education in college, working part-time in day-care centers.

After graduation, Karrie got a full-time job at a day-care center, working her way up to assistant manager. She kept working after her children were born, enjoying the added bonus of being able to bring her own kids to the center each day. When she and her husband moved from Alabama to Georgia after the birth of their fourth child, Karrie decided to strike out on her own. She spent time researching her new community and found that the only available child care was very expensive. She knew that while part of the community was affluent, a significant portion of the residents could not afford such expensive child care, and she decided to offer a more affordable option.

Karrie talked with the pastor of her church, who agreed that affordable day care for members of the congregation was a good idea. She applied to the local authorities for the necessary licensing and before long was operating a day-care center for twelve children in the church hall. In keeping with regulations, she hired one full-time and two part-time assistants. She pays a small portion of her monthly earnings as rent to the church.

Karrie is thrilled with her business. Although the days are long—the center is open from 6:30 A.M. until 7:00 P.M.—she loves being with children and having her own kids with her during the day. She can arrange her schedule so that one of her assistants closes up and Karrie can be at home for dinner with her family, as long as she is on call in case an emergency arises. "I love being able to help other members of the congregation and to earn some money doing what

I really enjoy," she says. "Although this is a small day-care center, it's enough for now because I enjoy it so much."

Information about offering child-care services is available from these sources: National Child Care Association at www.nccanet.org; National Association of Child Care Professionals at www.naccp.org; and Canadian Child Care Federation at www.cccf-fcsge.ca.

Services for the Elderly

The elderly and those confined to their homes alone can also use the services of someone who can look in on them regularly. Many of these people need someone reliable who can come in daily to clean their homes, go shopping, care for pets, perhaps cook one or two meals, bring in the mail, go to the bank, and take care of other errands. Some may even appreciate a morning check-up call to make certain all is well. Names of potential clients can be obtained from churches, senior citizen centers, and other community agencies. If you can establish a large enough clientele, you'll most likely have to employ several competent people to service your various clients.

A central coordinating service could also be welcome in the right setting, particularly in a community with many elderly residents. Tom O'Connor is a construction worker who lives in a close-knit hamlet of a suburban New York town. When he bought his small house four years ago and began to renovate it, he noticed a number of elderly neighbors taking an interest in his progress. The older men liked watching Tom's construction project, and the women enjoyed seeing his two-year-old daughter playing outside. Some offered meals to Tom and his wife after long days working on the house.

Tom has always felt comfortable with older people and appreciated his neighbors' kindness. He and his wife began to help an elderly couple who could no longer drive, taking them to weekend appointments and offering to pick up groceries when they went shopping. Soon after moving into the renovated house, Tom was laid off from his construction job. While he was looking for a new project and hoping to be called for work by his union, he found that he was spending a good deal of time helping his neighbors.

At first he did small repair jobs himself, and when a neighbor had an electrical problem, Tom asked a friend who is an electrician to look at the job. This gave Tom an idea. Since he worked in construction, he had acquaintances in most of the trades that a home owner would require. He knew plumbers, electricians, landscapers, roofers, painters—basically he or one of his friends would be able to address almost any issue a home owner might have.

Tom and his wife, who was becoming familiar with the community through activities with her daughter, put their heads together. They came up with a list of repair and service technicians for home, auto, and even personal services such as a hairstylist and manicurist. Tom printed a flyer that he distributed to private homes and a local senior citizens' residence and took out an ad in the local *Pennysaver*. When a client needs a service, he or she contacts Tom directly, and Tom makes the arrangements for the appropriate person to handle the situation. Tom is paid 8 percent of the fee received by the person who does the job.

The best part of this service for Tom is the ability to help his neighbors. It also provides some supplemental income during those times when construction work is slow.

From Hobby to Enterprise

Do you have a hobby that you enjoy spending time on, something that you've come to know a great deal about? If you do, you might want to consider it as a possible basis for your service career. A hobby can change the direction of your life, just as it did for Hazel and Glen Sigafoose of Montezuma, Iowa.

Hazel was a young dental assistant and Glen was a linotype operator (a linotype machine uses a ninety-character keyboard to create an entire line of metal type at once). When Glen was promoted to shop foreman, his bride, Hazel, took over his linotype job. They dreamed of one day owning their own newspaper.

In the meantime, Glen, who had been interested in model airplanes since childhood, saw a need for a service to provide balsa wood for modelers in the area who had no access to hobby shops. An advertisement in a model magazine brought immediate responses. Glen spent evenings cutting wood in the basement so Hazel could fill and pack the orders. Hazel's mother worked full-time on the project.

Four years later, Hazel and Glen left their newspaper jobs to erect their first building and hire three full-time employees. They started making airplane kits, and every two or three years they found they needed more manufacturing space. Their labor force grew to eighty-five employees in what began as a small supply service.

SIG Manufacturing Company Inc. became well known to airplane modelers. Unfortunately, Glen was killed in an air-show crash, but Hazel has carried on as president and owner. Today SIG still operates out of Montezuma, where employees in an eighty-thousand-square-foot facility manufacture more than two thousand products that are shipped to customers around the world.

Yearbook Photography

Robert Elkins became a photography bug at age nine. After graduating from a large Midwestern high school, he worked for a photography studio for three years and left when he was appointed his alma mater's yearbook photographer. Seven years later, Robert was photographing yearbooks for nine high schools and one junior college, a total of some seven thousand students. He doesn't charge a fee and, in fact, gives each parent-teacher association a percentage of his profits. All of his income is from the sale of graduation photographs to individual students.

Robert had to build a studio, buy equipment, and hire five full-time employees to help with the work. The greatest problem he sees is keeping track of every student's negatives and orders, prints, payments, and correspondence, all of which requires a huge record-keeping and filing system. His statistics suggest the work is worth it: seven thousand students of whom 70 percent, or forty-nine hundred, purchase various picture assortments. Naturally he has to deduct expenses from these sales, but his net profit isn't bad!

Offshore Sailing School

If you love the water and have the right skills, you might be interested in a business offering sailing instruction. Steve Colgate taught sailing on City Island, New York, and eventually married Doris, one of his first students.

The couple moved to Captiva Island, Florida, where they established Colgates' Offshore Sailing School. A fleet of boats and instructors enabled the company to offer a wide range of courses, including special sessions for doctors under a seminar program sponsored by the American Medical Association.

Today the Colgates have operations in ten locations in the United States and the Caribbean. The schools offer lessons and certifications in all levels of sailing ability. More than one hundred thousand people have graduated from Colgate courses.

Theatrical Agent and Personal Management

One glamorous service business that you might be interested in pursuing is that of theatrical agent or personal manager. Both call for a person with special talents, many contacts, and a wide knowledge of show business. An agent, who may work either alone or for a theatrical booking agency, represents a performing artist and handles all arrangements involved in booking the artist for performances. On the other hand, a personal manager uses her or his knowledge and contacts to advance a client's career. This may include making records, acting in a television series or special, obtaining publicity, making personal appearances, or playing a lead in a play or movie.

If you are interested in one of these occupations, your best bet is to find a job with a theatrical booking agency. That's the first step Wally Amos took on his way to becoming Famous Amos. Granted, you probably won't end up becoming a famous celebrity and head of an international cookie company, but you never know where the road might lead.

Famous Amos

One afternoon more than two thousand men, women, and children pushed their way into an attractively decorated store on the corner of Hollywood's Sunset Boulevard and Formosa, and then jammed a nearby courtyard. They had been invited to a party marking the debut of Famous Amos Chocolate Chip Cookies, where they enjoyed music, champagne, and tray after tray of freshly baked chocolate chip cookies.

The road to this party started when Wally Amos was twelve. When his parents separated and his mother decided he would be better off with relatives in New York than in his native Tallahassee,

Florida, she packed her son some food and put him on a train headed north to live with his aunt in New York City. One of his greatest pleasures was when his aunt baked her delicious chocolate chip cookies.

Wally worked at several jobs before finding his career, from the stockroom at Saks Fifth Avenue to the William Morris mail room. Once he worked his way up to becoming a theatrical agent, he dealt with such performers as Simon and Garfunkel, Diana Ross, and Marvin Gaye. Later, he resigned to open his own personal management firm for performers and celebrities. There were prosperous times that included travel and fine living, followed by lean years with little or no income. It was during this slow time that he started thinking about how much he missed his aunt's home-baked cookies. A friend's offhand suggestion that he establish a cookie business galvanized him into action.

Once he had launched his business, Wally found that baking and selling cookies didn't at all resemble running a service business such as personal management. The first serious problem to solve was learning how to mass produce the cookies without losing the flavor of home baking, which is done in small quantities. Just as important was the question of how to market the cookies with limited capital.

A friend introduced Wally to a buyer at New York's Bloomingdale's department store, and "Famous Amos" opened bakeries in the twelve Bloomingdale's stores on the East Coast and began selling in university campus stores all over the country. It became a worldwide operation, doing a multimillion-dollar business.

In fact, Famous Amos became so famous that the shirt and hat Wally wore in the photo on his cookie bag are on exhibit in the Business Americana collection of the Smithsonian's National

Museum of American History, the first food company and the first black businessman to be represented there.

Wally Amos also believes in service of another kind. He has served on the board of the Friends of Libraries, U.S.A., which is affiliated with the American Library Association. He has traveled widely on behalf of Literacy Volunteers of America, helping to open reading centers and visiting prisons. He uses his cookies as a reward for children who learn to read, telling them, "If you can't read, you can't succeed." Putting it another way, he says, "If I hadn't known how to read, I never would have started Famous Amos Cookies."

A Final Word

The businesses discussed in this chapter represent only some of the options for services geared toward individuals. Use these examples as a starting point, or be creative and think about what the residents of your community might be lacking. You never know where you'll get the inspiration for a service business that lots of people might be waiting for.

14

How About a Franchise?

You may not realize it, but you encounter franchise businesses just about every day. You've probably patronized one or more, perhaps even on a regular basis. For example, if your day includes coffee at Dunkin' Donuts, a visit to the Ace Hardware store for paint, a stop at CardSmart for some wrapping paper, lunch at Subway, dropping off a package at The Mail Box Store, and an afternoon treat at Carvel, you've visited six franchises.

If you want to operate your own service business but aren't completely ready to go it alone, franchising can be an excellent alternative. As you'll read in this chapter, there are certain advantages to buying a franchise that other business owners don't have.

What Is Franchising?

A franchise is an agreement between a business owner and a parent company that gives the owner the right to sell or distribute the company's products or services. The store or business itself is also called a *franchise*.

There are more than fifteen hundred franchises in the United States and twelve hundred in Canada, with thousands of franchisees operating businesses across North America. The industry generates billions of dollars each year and continues to grow.

Advantages and Disadvantages of Franchising

As with any business venture, it's important to consider both the pros and cons of franchising before making a commitment.

Advantages

Owning a franchise has several advantages for you as a service business owner. One of the main advantages of buying a franchise is its brand recognition. You'll be opening a business that already has an established reputation and customer base, making it that much easier to attract people.

The franchisor (parent company) may provide help in obtaining financing, setting up an accounting system, and planning marketing and promotional campaigns. You will generally receive training from the franchisor. McDonald's trains its new franchisees at Hamburger University, with locations in seven countries.

The franchisor may help choose a location, obtain financing, set up the accounting system, and plan marketing and promotional campaigns. Some franchise opportunities are turnkey operations, meaning that your investment gets you a completely stocked, ready-to-run business. Because the service is standardized, customers come to you with a sense of confidence, so you benefit from the franchisor's experience and avoid start-up mistakes. You have a ready-made business, which saves you many of the headaches and problems that come from establishing your own enterprise.

You can buy a franchise individually or with a partner, which can lessen your financial obligation. And if you are financially able to, you can own more than one franchise.

Disadvantages

To fully evaluate whether a franchise is the right venture for you, you must also consider the possible disadvantages of entering into this type of business arrangement.

As a franchisee your contract stipulates that you agree to run your business according to the franchisor's rules and regulations. These cover operating methods, accounting, territory limitations, and the schedule of commissions (also called royalties) to be paid back to the franchisor.

You may be required to purchase all or some of the products you use or sell from the franchisor. Even if you know of a source that offers a better-quality product or the same quality at a lower price, you cannot buy it from that source.

If you find that you disagree with some of the prescribed financing or operating methods, you must abide by your contract and follow the franchisor's regulations. Even if you see a way in which you can increase your business by adopting an innovative idea, it is possible that it won't be allowed.

These disadvantages don't seem to stop many people from entering the franchise industry. In Canada alone, franchising creates one billion jobs and generates approximately $116 billion annually. If you do the research and thoroughly investigate your options, chances are that the advantages of owning a franchise will far outweigh the disadvantages.

What Does a Franchise Cost?

There is a wide variety of investment options for potential franchisees. Some franchises can be obtained for $50,000 or less, but many cost upward of $500,000, depending on the investment required for property, building, furnishings, equipment, stock, and so forth. Don't let these numbers stagger or discourage you if you have limited resources. Depending on your personal resources, it is possible to get a bank loan or mortgage, and many franchisors are also prepared to help with financing.

There are some excellent Internet resources where you can find available franchises in the United States and Canada that fit your financial situation. Visit www.franchise.com to browse franchises by investment amount, location, or category. You can also find information about potential lenders and attorneys, as well as a net worth calculator and currency converter.

Another useful site is www.entrepreneur.com, which provides a wealth of information about entrepreneurship in general as well as specific resources for anyone considering a franchise.

You might also consider talking with the owner of a franchise. He or she is probably protected from competition within a given area and so may be willing to share valuable information that will enable you to judge whether you should pursue the matter further.

Should You Become a Franchisor?

So far we've been considering the possibility of becoming a franchisee. But what if your business idea is so successful that *you* end up becoming a franchisor? Although that might seem like quite a big dream right now, it does happen. Or perhaps you already have an idea for a business that would profit from the franchise format. Read the following accounts to see that success is possible.

1-800-GOT-JUNK?

If you've already begun to research and plan your service business career by reading publications such as the *Wall Street Journal, Fortune,* or *Business Week,* or if you watch CNN or "Oprah," chances are you've already encountered the story of Brian Scudamore, founder of one of the fastest-growing companies in North America.

Right out of high school, Brian went into business in his hometown of Vancouver, British Columbia. He had $700 and an old pickup truck and charged a fee to haul away trash not picked up by the local sanitation department. He dropped out of school his last year at university to pursue his idea of franchising the company.

The company grew in the Vancouver area over the next few years, and by 1998 Brian decided to expand beyond his local area. He set a goal of placing his company in the top thirty metropolitan areas of North America within five years. Brian met that goal and continues to set additional goals based on his initial concept for the organization.

Today 1-800-GOT-JUNK? has more than two hundred franchisees throughout North America, maintaining a presence in most large cities. Its revenues in 2005 were $68 million, up more than 90 percent from the previous year.

Beau Jo's Restaurants

Franklyn W. Bair Jr. has been a natural entrepreneur since he was in the third grade, when he started an insurance service, insuring a little girl's toy piano. She tried to collect on the policy when the piano broke, but Frank refused to pay, pointing out that she hadn't paid the premium. Then he insured other children for five to ten cents a month. When he was nine he hired friends to mow yards and shovel sidewalks under his direction. As a tenth grader he was operating a small vending machine business and at fifteen became head busboy in a Duluth restaurant. Studies at the Universities of Michigan and Colorado, followed by a varied sales career, all helped prepare him for the next big step—one April first.

"That was no April Fool's joke," he says, "when I purchased the Beau Jo's, a pizza restaurant in Idaho Springs, Colorado, for $8,500 that I had scraped together and borrowed."

The restaurant had twenty-five seats and a single counter, and Frank and one part-time assistant were the only employees. Frank worked sixteen to eighteen hours every day of the week, and the restaurant grossed under $2,000 a month. During the early years, he and his assistant took home a combined income of $10,000.

Frank persevered and, two years after opening, expanded by franchising his restaurant concept to a group that opened a second Beau Jo's in Denver. Four years later he canceled the franchise and closed the Denver restaurant because of negligence on the part of the franchisee. He assumed all debts and back taxes and reopened the restaurant—an expensive but valuable learning experience. Two years later he formed B.J. Management to handle the administrative needs of the two establishments and gradually built up enough staff to provide broad management supervision and controls as he developed plans for future expansion to new sites.

After ten years in business, the original Beau Jo's Pizza, now in a new location, had two hundred seats, a payroll of $200,000, and sales climbing at an average of 105 percent each year. Frank attributes part of his success to the willingness to change, whether it's the decor of the restaurant or the location of his headquarters. He says, "A good businessman doesn't stand still. He looks ahead, and through change and experimentation he grows and improves the quality of what he does."

Today, after more than thirty years in business, the original Beau Jo's Pizza seats more than seven hundred customers and occupies four storefronts on a busy street. There are currently six franchise locations that employ more than 350 people.

Frank believes that the franchise system is an excellent means of providing superior dining service to the public. His experience in starting small and growing slowly is proof that franchising can be done with little initial capital and a lot of hard work.

A Final Word

If you think a franchise is an intriguing business idea, consult some of the books listed in the Suggested Reading for more information on this topic. Visit the franchise websites mentioned earlier in this chapter, www.franchise.com and www.entrepreneur.com, where you can find information on every aspect of the franchise industry.

15

PROVIDING SERVICES TO OTHER BUSINESSES

So FAR WE'VE discussed a variety of services that you might offer to individuals. But as you do your research and think about markets you can serve, don't forget about other businesses.

Unless they are huge conglomerates, most businesses are not self-sufficient. And as the number of small businesses grows throughout the United States and Canada, the market for services that they need expands as well. Just look at most of the businesses mentioned throughout this book, and you'll see that each of them requires the services of other companies. A restaurant owner needs to have menus printed and linens laundered, electricians and service technicians need business cards, insurance companies and real estate agents need stationery and preprinted forms. And those are only a few ideas. Even Fortune 500 companies can use the services of an innovative entrepreneur, as you'll see in this chapter.

So, where do business owners turn for the services they need? To other business owners, of course. This is an excellent way to build a network of local professionals who support one another's endeavors and send customers each others' way.

ASK Computer Systems, Inc.

Sandra Kurtzig started her business in a corner of her home with just $2,000 in savings and an idea. Her plan was to run a part-time business, but ASK Computer Systems soon grew out of the home and into the marketplace.

Sandra has degrees in engineering and marketing and had previously worked in a technical sales position. She started her company as a way to occupy her time while at home raising her family. Her first assignment was from a weekly newspaper that wanted her to put their deliverers' accounts on her computer to track them more easily. This went so well that she called on local manufacturers and soon was keeping records of purchases and sales, parts inventories, and other business data.

The company grew so quickly that Sandra could no longer handle it herself, but she had no trouble finding employees among computer majors about to graduate from Stanford University. She offered competitive salaries and stock options and had plenty of staff to handle the company's accounts. The students wrote the computer programs and it was Sandra's responsibility to sell them.

The part-time business went public, the value of its stock having tripled since it was issued two years before. Sales were $35 million and profits 10 percent of that figure. Sandra and her two hundred employees were then working in an office complex in Los Altos, California.

Sandra attributes her success in part to avoiding the temptation to diversify. She chose instead to concentrate on computer software programs only for manufacturing companies. This may be a wise policy for other new service entrepreneurs to keep in mind.

In addition to ASK Computer Systems, Sandra owns a second company with her son Andy. In 1996 they started eBenefits, a company that links small businesses to human resources, payroll, and benefits management services via the Internet. Using the services offered by eBenefits, employees use the Web to compare and select health benefits, insurance plans, payroll deductions, and mutual funds for their 401(k) plans.

Agricultural Services

Agriculture is one of our largest and most important industries. Many activities associated with it are in sales or manufacturing. Although the output of farming itself is products, not services, there are still many services related to agriculture that may provide interesting opportunities. Crop dusting services, planting and harvesting services, well digging and water testing and treatment, soil testing, stock breeding and artificial insemination services are but a few.

Agricultural services offer the opportunity to work outdoors in rural areas with a wide variety of people, plants, and animals. We will examine one such service that may prove surprising to urban dwellers who take their milk and cream very much for granted.

Artificial Insemination

This is a service business that is a possibility for someone who likes to work with animals and people, is willing to learn the technique of artificial insemination, and is ready to sell the service. Best of all, it is an opportunity for those who want to be outdoors in an agricultural occupation at a time when farming jobs are fast disappearing from the scene.

Joel Bartholomew, a professional in this unusual service industry, explains its advantages. "Farming is changing like everything else," he says. "Bulls used to 'service' the cows in the herd naturally. Now a large percentage of cows are bred artificially by a technician using frozen semen. The advantages of artificial insemination are that it is safer—a farmer no longer has to keep a dangerous bull on the farm, it avoids disease being transmitted from one animal to another, and it can effect genetic improvement in the herd, which in turn can increase milk production and life span of the cattle."

Joel, who lives in New York's upstate Herkimer County where much of New York City's milk is produced, dropped out of college because he disliked the prospect of working at a desk as an engineer, which had been his initial plan. By the end of his sophomore year, he thought he would rather earn a living outdoors and that he would like to work with animals.

He hired out on several farms to gain experience in dairying until he was able to have his own farm with a small herd. However, to pay his bills, Joel soon realized that he needed more cows than he could afford, so he decided to try the artificial insemination industry. He received the necessary training and equipment from a company that provides this service and then went out on his own.

Today Joel and his family live on their own farm. He handles the sales of semen to people who breed their own dairy cattle and has also lined up associates who handle sales and the artificial insemination service for those farmers who choose not to do it on their own.

Joel spends part of his time calling on farmers to make sure they are pleased with his services. He also acts as a consultant when a farmer needs advice and supervises his associates who are on call. In addition to his artificial insemination services, Joel also has a service sales operation that provides farmers with dairy supplies.

Joel believes in the importance of artificial insemination to the farming community and feels that this is a service business worth investigating. There are a number of companies that provide the training and equipment you'll need to build your own business.

If this field interests you but you don't have farm experience, Joel urges you to investigate the opportunities in your area. Talk with representatives from some of the artificial insemination companies and/or the county farm agent to determine what you should do to prepare yourself for a job in this field. Check the yellow pages under "Artificial Insemination" or run an Internet search for companies in your area.

Morale Boosters

Laura J. Stoll worked for eight years as a management consultant for a major firm. As her career progressed, she began traveling full-time to meet with corporate clients throughout the United States and Europe.

When she decided she wanted to travel less, she accepted a job with another company that turned out to be an extremely unpleasant experience. She found herself working in a very negative environment where change was unwelcome and the management style was oppressive. Laura resigned from this position after only eight months, promising herself that she would never again be so unhappy with her job.

During this time, Laura became familiar with the world of corporate entertainment through her husband's work as an improvisational actor. She found that she had lots of creative ideas about this area and began thinking about how they might form the basis of a new business. The only good thing to come from her last corporate job was the push it gave her toward taking the leap and beginning her own company.

Laura founded The Riot Act, which offers services designed to make corporate meetings more effective, engaging, and fun. The company's services vary based on the needs of clients and include improvisational acting performances, team-building exercises, facilitated discussions, and training in interactive sessions. She has a staff of professional actors who work to energize employees and thereby improve performance and productivity.

The Riot Act has performed services for global corporations and Fortune 500 companies. Laura coordinates all activities and performances, looks for new clients, and researches materials needed for various activities. After a year in business, the company is thriving. Having outgrown their small home office, Laura and her husband recently rented a professional space that can accommodate their growing business.

Looking Up

Sometimes it seems as if new stores are being built all around us. Strip malls appear on stretches of commercial road, new supermarkets open in growing neighborhoods, and schools are built to accommodate expanding communities. You might not be aware of it, but each of these new construction projects provides work for service professionals in a number of trades, from hanging drywall to painting to electrical work to supplying signage.

David Scanlon is an acoustical ceiling contractor. His company, Tri State Acoustics Corp., is hired to install ceiling tiles on commercial projects. He has worked in stores, offices, hospitals, schools, and churches on both new construction jobs and renovations of existing buildings.

Tri State Acoustics is a good example of how a relatively small company can provide services to big clients. A family-owned business, Tri State's only permanent employees are David and his son. Together they seek out new projects, read the blueprints for the job, and prepare an estimate of how much to charge for their work. If the bid is accepted, they order materials and plan their work schedule. There are a few employees they hire on a temporary basis as projects come up. Given the nature of the construction business, many workers move from job to job rather than work for one full-time employer, and so they are often available on short notice if they've recently finished another project. Construction is also a highly unionized industry, so David can call the local union hall to request members who are looking for work from the union's ranks.

Working on a tightly organized schedule that allows each trade to complete its work in a timely manner, David and his crew install the metal grid system that will support the ceiling tiles and later install the specially ordered tiles into the grid. Although this might not sound like a great deal of work, in a new school that has more than two hundred thousand square feet of ceiling space, this type of job can last for months. In addition, many new projects call for tiles that are very delicate or oddly shaped, which require skill and precision in installation.

David has always worked in some form of service industry. When he was discharged from the navy thirty years ago, he started a home renovation business in his suburban New York community. He later formed a construction company with his brother Mike, and they began to specialize in acoustical ceiling installation. They ran a successful business together for ten years until Mike decided to move out of state. By this time David's eldest son, who had worked part-time with his father for several years, was about to graduate from high school. He came aboard as a full-time employee and after twelve years became his father's partner in the business.

David maintains an office in his home, where he can work on blueprints and job estimates and order materials. His wife helps with the office work, preparing estimates and invoices and handling the bank accounts. He doesn't stock any inventory of ceiling materials because each job calls for a specific tile. The company does maintain a supply of expensive tools, including an electronic laser used for achieving a level line, scaffolds, and an assortment of power tools.

David says that he can't imagine having spent his career doing any other work, even though there have been lean times when new work was hard to find and all the payments from completed jobs had already been deposited in the bank. He loves being self-employed, despite the occasional setbacks and difficulties, and enjoys seeing his finished products in many local establishments. When asked what he feels makes his company a success, he says, "Getting up one more time after you've been knocked down."

Typography

When Cynthia Solis's employer, a publishing firm, went bankrupt, she arranged to purchase the typesetting equipment with time payments and rented a small store in the northwest section of Chicago. At first she did everything herself, working sixteen to eighteen hours every day selling her service, setting type, delivering jobs, doing her own accounting, and even sweeping the floor. Six years later, Picatype Inc. had sales of more than $250,000, although the business was still operating out of one shop. Cynthia was satisfied to limit expansion to what could be handled in one location rather than open new branches.

Perhaps she summed up in four words what the first chapters of this book have been stressing: "Service is what counts."

Freight-Delivery Service

Sun City was an eight-company trucking complex based in El Paso, Texas. Marie Tarvin Garland purchased a small local freight-delivery service consisting of one customer and a small van. She borrowed a desk and chair for her office and went to work soliciting business. It wasn't easy because people didn't take her seriously as a woman running a trucking company. The first year she lost $4,000, but fortunately she also had income from a bar she owned and operated. After a couple of years, the air-freight forwarders discovered her and then business began to grow. Today a labor force of one hundred employees, including some forty women, and more than sixty trucks attest to Marie Garland's tenacity.

Importance of Innovation

How many times have you used a copy machine? We can't even imagine a time when it wasn't possible to make multiple copies of a document in a matter of minutes. But believe it or not, the first potential customers to whom Xerox showed their new machine weren't interested! Everyone anticipated a very small market, perhaps a few thousand machines, not enough to justify the initial required investment. These businesspeople saw the machines as only being used to make a copy or two of a letter. No one was farsighted enough to see the real potential—that copy machines could make copies of everything, not just correspondence. That eventually it could also produce four-color copies for countless different printing projects.

So, what does this have to do with your service business career? Possibly everything. Throughout this book you've read about various business ideas, some that are fairly traditional and some that were rather risky. The point is that ideas come from many places, sometimes where and when you'd least expect. Given today's technology and the rate at which society experiences change, don't be afraid to dream.

Innovation is the basis of many businesses. Don't dismiss any of your ideas as too far-fetched or impossible. When you come up with something new, spend some time with the idea. Analyze it, research it, follow the steps that have been outlined in this book, and you might find yourself with a successful new career.

Suggested Reading

THE FOLLOWING BOOKS should prove helpful in starting a service business of your own. You should also check to see what books your local college, public, and school libraries have in their respective collections. Also consult the *Reader's Guide to Periodical Literature* and the subject volume of *Books in Print*.

Addison, Lisa. *Start Your Own Personal Concierge Service.* Irvine, Calif.: Entrepreneur Media Inc., 2002.

Andrews, Lynda. *The Food Service Professionals Guide to Series: Buying and Selling a Restaurant Business: For Maximum Profit.* Ocala, Fla.: Atlantic Publishing Group, 2003.

Ball, Victoria Kloss. *Opportunities in Interior Design and Decorating Careers*, 2nd ed. Chicago: McGraw-Hill, 2001.

Bell, Chip, and Ron Zemke. *Service Magic: The Art of Amazing Your Customers.* Chicago: Dearborn Trade Publishing, 2003.

Birkeland, Peter M. *Franchising Dreams: The Lure of Entrepreneurship in America.* Chicago: University of Chicago Press, 2002.

Boyette, Donna Dickason. *How to Make Money While You Look for a Job: Start a Very Small Service Business on a Shoestring—A Step-by-Step Workbook*. Bangor, Maine: Booklocker.com Inc., 2005.

Brown, Bruce Cameron. *How to Use the Internet to Advertise, Promote, and Market Your Business or Website with Little or No Money*. Ocala, Fla.: Atlantic Publishing Group Inc., 2006.

Brown, Douglas Robert. *The Restaurant Managers Handbook: How to Set Up, Operate, and Manage a Financially Successful Food Service Operation*, 3rd ed. Ocala, Fla.: Atlantic Publishing Group, 2003.

Burns, Julie Kling. *Opportunities in Computer Careers*. Chicago: McGraw-Hill, 2002.

Coleman, Ronny J. *Opportunities in Fire Protection Services Careers*, 2nd ed. Chicago: McGraw-Hill, 2003.

DeWalt, Suzanne. *How to Start a Home-Based Interior Design Business*, 3rd ed. Guilford, Conn.: Globe Pequot, 2003.

Donovan, Mary. *Opportunities in Culinary Careers*, 2nd ed. Chicago: McGraw-Hill, 2004.

Durst, Christine, and Michael Haaren. *The 2-Second Commute: Join the Exploding Ranks of Freelance Virtual Assistants*. Franklin Lakes, N.J.: Career Press, 2005.

Edwards, Kenneth W. *Your Successful Real Estate Career*, 5th ed. New York: American Management Association, 2006.

Ennen, Diana, and Kelly Poelker. *Virtual Assistant, the Series: Becoming a Highly Successful, Sought-After VA*, 2nd ed. O'Fallon, Ill.: Another 8 Hours Publishing, 2004.

Erickson, Mandy. *Start Your Own Executive Recruiting Business*. Irvine, Calif.: Entrepreneur Media Inc., 2003.

Field, Shelly. *Career Opportunities in the Music Industry*, 5th ed. New York: Checkmark Books, 2004.

Fine, Janet. *Opportunities in Teaching Careers*, 2nd ed. Chicago:
    McGraw-Hill, 2005.

Foote, Cameron S. *The Creative Business Guide to Running a
    Graphic Design Business*, 2nd ed. New York: W.W. Norton,
    2004.

Gearhart, Susan Wood. *Opportunities in Beauty and Modeling
    Careers*. Chicago: McGraw-Hill, 2004.

Goerl, William J. *Wheels of Gold: A Complete How-to Guide for
    Starting a Million Dollar Limousine Business*. Bay Shore, N.Y.:
    Paradise Planning Inc., 2004.

Gregg, M. Scott. *Profitable Plumbing: How to Make the Most
    Money in the Plumbing and Heating Trade*. Bloomington, Ind.:
    AuthorHouse, 2004.

Harper, Stephen C. *The McGraw-Hill Guide to Starting Your Own
    Business: A Step-by-Step Blueprint for the First-Time
    Entrepreneur*, 2nd ed. Chicago: McGraw-Hill, 2003.

Henkin, Shepard. *Opportunities in Hotel and Motel Careers*, 2nd
    ed. Chicago: McGraw-Hill, 2006.

Jamison, Michelle. *The Virtual Assistant's Guide to Marketing*.
    Tarentum, Pa.: Word Association, 2003.

Kimball, Cheryl. *Start Your Own Pet-Sitting Business*. Irvine,
    Calif.: Entrepreneur Media Inc., 2004.

Kirkland, Susan. *Start and Run a Creative Services Business*.
    Bellingham, Wash.: Self-Counsel Press, 2005.

Krumhansl, Bernice R. *Opportunities in Physical Therapy Careers*,
    2nd ed. Chicago: McGraw-Hill, 2005.

LaRusic, Joel. *Start and Run a Landscaping Business*. Bellingham,
    Wash.: Self-Counsel Press, 2005.

Lewis, Jerre G. *How to Start and Manage an Answering Service
    Business*. Interlochen, Mich.: Lewis and Renn Associates,
    2004.

Lewis, Jerre G. *How to Start and Manage a Pest Control Service Business: A Practical Way to Start Your Own Business.* Interlochen, Mich.: Lewis and Renn Associates, 2004.

Lewis, Jerre G. *How to Start and Manage a Plumbing Service Business*, 2nd ed. Interlochen, Mich.: Lewis and Renn Associates, 2004.

Lewis, Jerre G. *How to Start and Manage a Tree Service Business: A Practical Way to Start Your Own Business*, 2nd ed. Interlochen, Mich.: Lewis and Renn Associates, 2004.

Lewis, Jerre G., and Leslie D. Renn. *How to Start and Manage a Carpet-Cleaning Service Business: A Practical Way to Start Your Own Business.* Interlochen, Mich.: Lewis and Renn Associates, 2004.

Lewis, Jerre G., and Leslie D. Renn. *How to Start and Manage a Temporary Help Services Business: A Practical Way to Start Your Own Business.* Interlochen, Mich.: Lewis and Renn Associates, 2005.

Lownes-Jackson, Millicent Gray. *Starting a Child Care Center: The Indispensable Guidebook for Starting a Day Care or Child Care Business.* Business of Your Own (TN), 2004.

Lynn, Jacqueline. *Start Your Own Business Support Service Business.* Irvine, Calif.: Entrepreneur Media Inc., 2003.

Lynn, Jacqueline. *Start Your Own Child-Care Service.* Irvine, Calif.: Entrepreneur Media Inc., 2006.

Lynn, Jacqueline. *Start Your Own Cleaning Service*, 2nd ed. Irvine, Calif.: Entrepreneur Media Inc., 2006.

Lynn, Jacqueline. *Start Your Own Senior Services Business.* Irvine, Calif.: Entrepreneur Media Inc., 2006.

McDonald, Matthew. *Creating Websites: The Missing Manual.* Sebastopol, Calif.: O'Reilly Media, 2005.

McLean, Cheryl. *Careers for Shutterbugs and Other Candid Types*, 2nd ed. Chicago: McGraw-Hill, 2002.

Milne, Robert, and Marguerite Backhausen. *Opportunities in Travel Careers*, 2nd ed. Chicago: McGraw-Hill, 2003.

Mitchell, Scott. *Create Your Own Website*, 2nd ed. Indianapolis: Sams Publishing, 2006.

Mucha-Aydlott, Julie. *How to Open Your Own In-Home Bookkeeping Service*, 2nd ed. Santee, Calif.: San Diego Business Accounting Solutions Inc., 2004.

Nelson, John Oliver. *Opportunities in Religious Service Careers*, 2nd ed. Chicago: McGraw-Hill, 2004.

Orenstein, Vik. *Photographers Market Guide to Building Your Photography Business: Everything You Need to Know to Run a Successful Photography Business*. Cincinnati: Writers Digest Books, 2004.

Parry, Chris. *The Food Service Professionals Guide to Bar and Beverage Operation: Ensuring Success and Maximum Profit*. Ocala, Fla.: Atlantic Publishing Group Inc., 2003.

Pinson, Linda. *Keeping the Books: Basic Record Keeping and Accounting for the Successful Small Business*, 6th ed. Chicago: Kaplan Business, 2004.

Pomerantz, Suzi. *Seal the Deal: The Essential Mindsets for Growing Your Professional Services Business*. Amherst, Mass.: HRD Press, 2007.

Ross, Stan. *The Inside Track to Careers in Real Estate*. Washington, DC: Urban Land Institute, 2006.

Ruskin-Brown, Ian. *Marketing Your Service Business*. London: Thorogood Publishing Ltd., 2005.

Sandlin, Eileen Figure. *Start Your Own Lawn Care Business*. Irvine, Calif.: Entrepreneur Media Inc., 2003.

Sawyer, Deborah C. *Smart Services: Competitive Information Strategies, Solutions, and Success Stories for Service Businesses.* Medford, N.J.: Cyberage Books, 2002.

Sims-Bell, Barbara. *Career Opportunities in the Food Industry and Culinary Professions*, 3rd ed. New York: Checkmark Books, 2007.

Teixeira, Ed. *Franchising from the Inside Out.* Philadelphia: Xlibris Corp., 2005.

Turner, Krista Thoren. *Start Your Own Staffing Service.* Irvine, Calif.: Entrepreneur Media Inc., 2004.

Turner, Marcia Layton. *The Unofficial Guide to Starting a Small Business*, 2nd ed. Hoboken, N.J.: Wiley, 2004.

Weeks, Zona R. *Opportunities in Occupational Therapy Careers*, 2nd ed. Chicago: McGraw-Hill, 2006.

Winovich, George. *Home Watch Services: A Guide for Starting Your Own Home-Based Business.* West Conshohocken, Pa.: InfinityPublishing.com, 2005.

ABOUT THE AUTHOR

ROBERT MCKAY WAS born in New York City, where he attended school, majoring in English, and later earning a B.S. in library science. He has had a variety of literary and business experience ranging from librarian, literary critic, writer, editor, and publisher, to private secretary, hotel manager, accountant, office manager, and corporate executive. The author of more than fifty-five books, he has written extensively in the field of vocational guidance. He is married and has three children and six grandchildren who constitute the most enthusiastic audience and the toughest critics for his writing.